ALI
WAS HERE

A promising life.
A brutal murder.
Justice, and a
legacy of hope.

James Kirkpatrick Davis

KANSAS CITY STAR BOOKS

Published by
Kansas City Star Books
1729 Grand Boulevard
Kansas City, MO 64108

Editor: Monroe Dodd
Designer: Jean Dodd

First Edition

ISBN: 978-1-935362-44-9
Library of Congress Control Number: 2009930566

Printed in the United States of America
by Walsworth Publishing Co., Inc.
Marceline, Mo.

Illustrations: Dust jacket, text pages i, ii, first through fourth photo pages
and bottom two on eighth photo page courtesy Roger and Kathy Kemp;
Fifth, sixth, seventh and top three on eighth photo page, *The Kansas City
Star.*

Contents

Foreword

John Walsh
"America's Most Wanted"

"John, this is horrible, really horrible! A young college girl — she was beaten to death at a public swimming pool. And John, the father discovered the body. It's real bad!"

The phone call was from Craig Hill, an old friend of mine. Craig was a major with the Leawood, Kansas, Police Department and a fierce advocate for child safety. When he got his teeth into something, he didn't let go.

"John, we don't have a clue. You've got to do this case!"

I called Lance Heflin, the executive producer of "America's Most Wanted" and my crime-fighting partner for nearly two decades. He would check out the case.

It didn't take long for Lance to nail down the details of the crime and make a decision. Not only was "America's Most Wanted" doing the case, we'd also travel to Kansas City to tape the show at the crime scene.

I was glad we were going, but it was also something I dreaded. Even though I've met with hundreds of parents who have lost a child to crime, it's always painful and never fails to reopen my own wound from the murder of my son, Adam.

Our schedule was rearranged and in no time the production crew was assembled at the swimming pool in Leawood. At one point, I was talking to one of the detectives working the case when Craig pulled me aside. In a low voice, he told me: "The father's here. John, this man has to talk to you. He's close to the edge." Then, Craig led me over to a light-haired man standing off by himself.

When I shook hands with Roger Kemp, the father of the murdered girl, I immediately noticed something familiar in his eyes — that haunted look of a man caught in a nightmare. It's desperation and torture and disbelief and anger and pain — all beyond measure. Only those who've been there can understand that hell.

Roger wanted to show me the pump room where the murder

had happened. Any normal person would have avoided going in there but I had no choice. I couldn't turn this man down.

Roger walked me through the crime scene, step by step, sparing me no detail of the murder. It was if talking about it would purge him of the horror and just make it all go away.

His 19-year-old daughter, Ali, had just finished her freshman year in college and was working at this small suburban pool for the summer. She was working alone when she was attacked. The killer beat Ali mercilessly. Then he strangled her. An hour later, Roger discovered his daughter's body.

Just as I feared, walking through the crime scene with Roger brought back everything about my own son's murder. It was hard enough to listen to Roger talk about Ali's murder, but resurrecting the pain from Adam's death was an additional punch in the gut. You've heard the old saying, "I cried that I had no shoes, until I met a man who had no feet." Well, standing next to Roger, I couldn't help thinking that this man was in even worse shape than I was after Adam's murder. God help him, the poor man had found his daughter's battered body!

As Roger talked, I kept thinking that this man is so badly damaged that there's no way I can help make it better. I can't make him less angry, less hurt, less broken-hearted. All I can do is offer him one thing. Just one thing: the possibility of getting justice.

And not "closure." I hate that word! Despite what pop psychologists say on TV, closure is never, ever possible. Roger would always carry in his mind the horrible sight of his dead daughter. And I know from bitter experience that the wound would never, ever fully heal.

I've always believed that if Adam, or any murdered child, could come back from the other side, even for just 30 seconds, he'd say:

"Don't destroy yourself. Be kind to Mom and the rest of the family. Please don't become a vigilante and take the law into your own hands. Honor my memory by doing things through the system, by changing the system. And don't let this consume you, don't let it destroy you. I'm in a better place and it will hurt me so much if my passing kills you too."

I think that's what I said to Roger, but I'm not sure. It was such a painful situation talking with him in that pump room. Considering what he'd been through, I honestly didn't expect much from Roger. I just hoped that he wouldn't become the killer's second victim.

The police had only two clues: a vague composite drawing of the killer and a description of his pickup truck. It wasn't much to go on, but "America's Most Wanted" aired the case on August 3, 2002, seven weeks after the murder. Tips poured in but there was no capture. Eight months later, we re-aired the case but again we got nothing. The scumbag was still out there.

People have asked me: "Why does Natalee Holloway get all the attention? Why did we hear Chandra Levy's name all the time and not the 5,000 other women who were also missing? Or the other 15,000 in the FBI computer?"

The answer is always the same: the parents. It's the parents who refuse to give up, who refuse to take "no" for an answer. Who don't listen to the overworked cop who says, "We don't have much chance of breaking this case." Or, "I'm overworked. I'm tired. And I have 50 other cases."

It's the parents who say to themselves, "If we're going to get the publicity to keep our child's name and unsolved case alive, we've got to saddle up."

My wife, Reve, said something to me soon after Adam was taken from us that I've never forgotten. It was during a very dark time when we were really hitting rock bottom. She said; "We're here dying of a broken heart, but we've forgotten who the real victim is. The real victim is Adam." Then, she looked me in the eye and said, "We've got to keep going." A short time later, Reve started the Adam Walsh Outreach Center for Missing Children out of our garage.

Roger Kemp is one of those extraordinary people who saddled up and got going. And with his family's support, he never gave up. He worked the Kansas City press to keep the case alive. And he never let up his quiet but steady pressure on the police investigators.

When the case stalled, Roger pressed on. One day, while driving to visit Ali's grave, Roger had an ingenious idea. He approached Lamar Advertising in Kansas City and told them he wanted to buy a billboard. Before long, the Lamar folks had designed and donated the billboard that Roger had in mind. It was the first "wanted" billboard. It showed the composite drawing of Ali's killer, a photo of the pickup truck, and a hotline number. As soon as it went up, that billboard generated tips.

But Roger didn't stop there. He thought, why not profile other fugitives? Working with the Kansas City police and Lamar, a "wanted" billboard profiling murderer Demetrius Gunnells was unveiled on March 17, 2004. Just four days later, that killer was in custody.

And so it began. Now, more than 40 cities are using "wanted" billboards and dozens of criminals are behind bars. Among them is Ali's killer, who was finally caught using tips from the billboard and "America's Most Wanted" viewers.

But Roger's works weren't done. He believed that if Ali had had just a little bit of an edge against her attacker she might have escaped. So he started The Ali Kemp Educational Foundation to give girls and women instruction in basic self-defense. In just three years. Roger and his team of instructors have trained more than 37,000 women across the country.

You know, parents of murdered children are members of a horrible club. It's as if we can see a certain color that others don't see. You can't explain it to them and you hope they never see it. Eighty percent of our marriages don't survive — further shattering families. Drugs and alcohol pull many of us down. The basics seem impossible — getting up in the morning, taking your vitamins, going to work and even loving the children you still have.

But these wounded parents don't have to fall apart and die from grief. They don't have to let the killer claim another victim. Roger Kemp is living proof of that. He hasn't allowed himself to be re-victimized. He hasn't taken his pain out on himself or his family. Instead, he's turned his hurt and anger into something positive and helpful to others.

Roger has tried to celebrate his daughter Ali and the precious 19 years he had with her. And I'm sure that whenever there are young women taking his self-defense classes, in each of their faces he sees a little bit of his daughter.

Roger's really making a difference in this country and I am extremely proud of him.

1

Day of Unreason

"It was hard to imagine that life could have been much better."
— Roger Kemp on his family's experience
before June 18, 2002

In 1922 Oscar J. Lee, a retired police officer from Oklahoma, bought up land along the Kansas-Missouri state line about 14 miles south of downtown Kansas City and established the roots of what would become Leawood, Kansas. It was incorporated as a city in 1948.

Since then, Leawood has grown to cover almost 15 square miles. In the last 25 years, its population has doubled to 32,000. Average household income is slightly more than $100,000, placing the city in the 98th percentile nationally. The median age is 41; money is plentiful; the average Leawood home is appraised at more than $450,000. Slightly more than 68 percent of residents have a college bachelor's degree or higher.

The city boasts tree-lined residential neighborhoods, wide boulevards, fashionable shopping centers, country clubs and recreation areas.

A police department was established in 1949, staffed at that time by unpaid volunteers. Until 1974, the tiny department operated out of three rooms in the basement of city hall. As Leawood has grown, so has the department, which is now on Lee Boulevard with a staff of 60 officers and 25 administrative personnel. Partly because of the department's innovative investigative programs and solid day-to-day police work, Leawood has been largely devoid of serious crime. Few homicides occur and only one, dating from 1981, remains unsolved.

Over the years, Leawood has proved a safe and secure

community. Its residents have advanced their careers, made a good living, raised families, volunteered, gone to church or synagogue, played sports, attended social functions and enjoyed the good life.

AT 9 O'CLOCK on the overcast morning of June 18, 2002, Roger Kemp departed his Leawood residence and headed for his office in the Corporate Woods office park.

Kemp worked as a manufacturer's representative for the company he had founded in 1974, Kemp & Associates, which markets injection-molding equipment and machinery to the plastics industry. Because several of his top customers were in California, he usually worked until 7 p.m.

For Roger and Kathy Kemp, these had been vintage years. Their large brick residence — which the Kemps designed themselves — was only a year old.

"This was our dream home," he says. "This was it.

"Some of our friends and people we knew had places in Florida or Arizona or a place at the lake, but our house on Mission Road was our castle. It was everything we could possibly have hoped for; it was an idyllic setting. With friends and family, and living in Leawood, it was hard to imagine that life could have been much better."

Kathy Kemp, born Kathy Bower, grew up in a rural area in southern Missouri about 30 miles north of the Arkansas border. Naturally gregarious, Kathy had always been popular. In her junior year at Carl Junction High School she was president of the Missouri Future Homemakers of America. She was a high school cheerleader and president of her senior class. At Southwest Missouri State in Springfield, she joined Alpha Delta Pi sorority. She received a master's degree in criminal behavior from the University of Missouri-Kansas City. For more than a decade after graduating from college, she worked as a state and later federal probation officer.

Two of Roger Kemp's college fraternity brothers were also probation officers; through them Roger met Kathy. They married in 1979.

Roger Kemp hailed from King City, a small town in northwest Missouri. In high school, he worked at the Ford plant in Claycomo, a Kansas City suburb, and continued to do so on Friday and Saturday nights in his years at Central Missouri State University.

"Ford treated me very well, and the extra money was great," he says. "Since I was majoring in industrial management, my boss said to get that degree and come back here and we will have a job waiting for you."

That didn't work out. When Kemp graduated, the recession of the early 1970s had set in, Ford was laying off workers and the job did not materialize. Instead, he went to work as a sales representative for a fiberglass-products manufacturer. He had never thought about becoming a salesman.

"After three months on the job, the president of the company called me into his office," Kemp says, "and told me I was doing a good job and that I was now the assistant sales manager and gave me a raise. I thought that was pretty neat." Three months later, the company president called Roger Kemp back to his office and said, "I have just fired the sales manager, and I want you to be the new sales manager." Kemp thought to himself at the time, "Either I am pretty good in sales or this man goes through sales managers like crazy."

A year and a half later Kemp got the urge to start his own company and founded Kemp & Associates. In the first three years, Kemp recalls, "We almost starved."

"It was constant travel throughout the Midwest, long, long hours, often 18-hour days."

Then his firm shifted strategy. It began to specialize in selling new injection-molding machines, taking old ones in trade, refurbishing them and re-selling them.

"At that time the idea had never been done, and we began to serve across the United States," he says. "The business just took off."

In 1982, Roger and Kathy Kemp had their first child, Alexandra Elizabeth Kemp. A boy, Tyler, was born in 1984 and another boy, Drew, in 1986. For a few years, Kathy returned to work and the Kemps hired a nanny to care for the children, but they didn't like that setup. Kathy became a full-time mother.

"That is the best decision we ever made," she says.

G ROWING UP, Alexandra became "Ali."

"She kept things going around the house all the time," Kathy recalls. Ali was almost always "up for something new." She loved to pester her brothers, and they sparred good-naturedly.

Ali played sports through her high school years at Blue Valley North in Leawood, as did Tyler and Drew. All three attended school with friends they had known all their lives. The Kemp home on Mission Road was often party headquarters.

"We had plenty of parties all those years on the lower level for one kid or another," Roger Kemp recalls. "For some reason, Ali's friends always came through the garage, Tyler's friends came through the front door and Drew's friends came though the back door. Sometimes all three groups were at the house at the same time. Those were fabulous years; we had so much to be thankful for."

At Blue Valley North High School, Ali was a Student Ambassador, member of the National Honor Society, co-president of Future Business Leaders of America and Student Council member. She served on the Sweetheart Court and in the Spirit Club and the Senior Rough Riders. She lettered in soccer for the Lady Mustangs.

Friends and acquaintances called her "a phenomenal person, always smiling, fun-loving, always with her head on straight." She made new friends everywhere she went and could balance academics with her many activities.

"She definitely was human with faults like all of us," her mother says. Ali "may not have been a 10 in any category — not the most beautiful, not the fastest, not the most athletic, not the most scholarly, but she was a 9 in virtually all of those categories. It is fair to say that Ali had the total package. She was a happy person, and that influenced everyone she knew."

Her high school principal, Richard Siebs, said she had "a poise that stood out for someone her age."

Ali Kemp graduated in 2001 and headed for Kansas State University in Manhattan, which is about 130 miles west of Leawood. Life on campus was much the same as at high school; she lived at the same rapid pace and every day was a gift. Her philosophy, friends and family said, was this: Tomorrow is not promised to any of us, so make the most of today.

She pledged Pi Beta Phi and was her sorority's Panhellenic representative on campus. She was selected for the Honors Program and the National Society of Collegiate Scholars, qualified as an Academic Scholar in the College of Human Ecology and finished the first year in the top 10 percent of her class. She planned to major in mass communications with a minor in public relations. Ali also found time to play intramural soccer and basketball.

As spring semester of her freshman year came to an end, Ali looked forward to August, to be on the "other side" of sorority rush for the first time. First, however, she had other choices to make. She had been invited to travel with about 60 other students from across the country to France, China and Australia on behalf of the State Department. In addition, a local church invited her to join their group to work with young people in Russia.

And before she made those choices, Ali's father encouraged her to take a summer job.

"We did not want Ali and her brothers to hang around the house all the time and ask mom and dad for money," he says. "We wanted them to go to work and learn what earning money was really like."

So for the second summer in a row, Ali hired on as a pool attendant at the Foxborough Community Pool at 123rd Street and State Line Road, about a mile from the Kemp home. Also signing up to work at the pool were her two brothers and her boyfriend of five years, Phil Howes, a student at the University of Kansas.

The pool is available to residents of the 300 homes in the Hunter's Ridge and Foxborough neighborhoods of Leawood. Besides a swimming pool, the Foxborough complex has a wading pool and two single-story buildings, beige with white trim along their roofs. One houses the pump and storage room, the other showers, restrooms and lockers.

The pump room, which measures 19 feet 3 inches by 18 feet 9 inches, contains the pool's water pumps and filtering system. It also holds extra chairs, which are stacked along the south wall, a first-aid kit, pool toys, a pool cover, a 50-foot vacuum hose and pole, cleaning supplies and chemicals.

The pool complex sits in the corner of an upscale Leawood neighborhood. It is bounded on two sides by high-traffic, multilane streets – on the east by State Line Road and the north by 123rd Street. Across State Line Road is Kansas City, Missouri. Across 123rd is a Leawood shopping center.

Access to the pool complex and its parking lot is by Pembroke Lane, a winding, two-lane street on the west side. The backyards of five single-family homes line the southern boundary of the complex.

A wrought-iron fence surrounds the immediate area of the pool. Along it grow shrubs and small trees. Outside the fence, pines and ornamental trees bound the pool property. Once spring arrives, heavy foliage makes it difficult to see the pool from adjacent streets and sidewalks.

IN THE SHOPPING CENTER across the street from the pool, a branch bank on the morning of June 18 served a stream of customers. Not far away, the Blue Hills golf course was hosting the annual Tom Watson Golf Tournament.

At 10 a.m. that day, Phil Howes opened the Foxborough pool. He unlocked the gates, cleaned up around the pool and outside areas and put the chairs in order.

Foxborough had no lifeguard or other employees, so the attendant typically worked alone. Duties included monitoring the flow of water and pool chemicals, cleaning the pool and restrooms, updating and initialing the attendants' task board and having visitors sign the pool register.

That morning, Phil put chemicals through the filtration system and back-flushed the system to clean it out. He opened the pool register, which was kept in a notebook that also listed the pool's work schedule for the week, and placed it on a work table near the front gate. Because the day began under overcast skies, few people came to the pool early on. Lawn-care workers trimmed shrubs and cut grass adjacent to the pool.

At 2 p.m., Ali Kemp arrived to take over the next shift. She and Phil chatted. Ali mentioned, as she had before, that the lawn-care workers sometimes made her nervous. Phil left the pool at 2:15

p.m.

Ordinarily, Ali's shift would have ended at 6 p.m., but she and Phil planned to go to dinner and a movie that evening. Ali arranged with her brother, Tyler, to take over her shift at 5 p.m.

At 2:51 p.m., Ali called Phil on her cell phone. By then, Phil was at work at another pool, and missed the call. Ali left a voice mail suggesting a movie they could see. Within a few minutes, she entered the pump room, which also served as storage for pool supplies, chairs and pool toys.

There were no other attendants at the time, and no pool patrons.

Phil noticed the missed call on his cell phone about 4 p.m. and returned it. There was no answer.

AT 2:55 P.M., a 1980s-vintage pickup truck pulled into the Foxborough pool parking lot. Out stepped the owner and sole employee of Hoover Pool Services, hoping to talk to someone about bidding for a maintenance contract. Cold-calling for prospects is a common practice in the pool service industry.

Pool suppliers knew the man as Ted Hoover, a 26-year-old who had begun his little company the year before and had assembled a clientele from homeowners in Leawood and other wealthy neighborhoods.

He parked his truck, picked up his five-gallon carryall bucket and walked through the front gate to the pool's edge. It was probably 3 p.m. when he turned and decided to check the pool's filters. He assumed they were in the pump room. Its big double doors were open. Seeing no one, he walked to the doorway and looked in.

There, for the first time in his life, he saw Ali Kemp. She was dressed casually in shorts and a T-shirt.

He found her stunningly attractive.

ALI KEMP'S CLOSE FRIEND, Laurel Vine, had a doctor's appointment that afternoon. Afterward, Laurel stopped by a Taco Bell at 103rd Street and State Line Road. She left the restaurant at 3:10 p.m. and drove her Honda Civic south on State Line.

Seeing Ali's Jeep in the parking lot of the Foxborough pool, she stopped there. It was about 3:15 p.m. Laurel noticed some of Ali's belongings on a table next to the pump room. That was where Ali usually left her things, and where she sometimes did homework.

Still sitting in her car, Laurel honked her horn to get Ali's attention. There was no response.

"Then I saw someone look over the table," she recalls. It was a man, about 5 feet 10 inches tall, "a white male with a little bit of a receding hairline."

"I thought he was saying something to Ali, so I thought that it might have been like a supervisor or maintenance worker who was going to tell that I was being obnoxious."

The man walked out of the pool area. She remembered him "wearing, like, coveralls...or a jumpsuit and grayish-blue color or blue."

The man saw Laurel in her car, waved, got into his pickup and drove away. Laurel got out of her car and walked in. Because Ali's things lay on the table, she assumed her friend had left briefly to get something to eat from the shopping center across the street. Nevertheless, Laurel looked in the pump room and called Ali's name. There was no response. Laurel scanned the pool area and the bathrooms and, finding no one, got back into her car and went home. Ali's friend remembered a red truck and "at least one worker mowing and doing some yard work around the pool."

About 3:17 p.m., Hunter's Ridge resident Tamara Baker was driving home from work. She stopped to check on the progress of her daughters, Elizabeth and Brittany, who were walking along the sidewalk about a block from the pool with three other girls. They were on their way for a swim. Tamara talked to them briefly, and then drove home to change clothes so she could go to the pool herself.

Arriving at the entrance, Elizabeth Baker signed the register for all five girls and they went swimming.

The pump room doors, they saw, were open. They went in and out several times to get pool toys. On one of those trips, 15-year-old Meredith Lindsey noticed several items on the table near the pump room entrance, including a water bottle, a Kansas State University notebook laid out with papers and a cell phone. The cell phone rang constantly.

Elizabeth and Meredith looked at the caller ID. Calls were coming from two people. They thought they might be from Ali's boyfriend and another friend. Meredith was about to pick up the phone and answer it, but Elizabeth urged her not to.

"She might come back in a minute and get mad if you are messing with her stuff," Elizabeth said. They put the phone down and went back to the pool.

When Elizabeth's mother arrived, she saw Ali's black Jeep in the parking lot.

"I did not notice anything unusual," Tamara Baker recalls. She saw no attendant, but that did not strike her as odd.

Some time before 3:30 p.m., Meredith's mother, Sheila Lindsey, a teacher in the Grandview School District, stopped by the pool with Meredith's swimming suit. Finding no attendant on duty, she wondered whether something was wrong.

"Mom," Meredith said, "everything is OK. Maybe she has gone off. Her car is right there. She'll be right back. Don't worry about it."

But Sheila Lindsey was not convinced. "There was no attendant on duty and that concerned me." She stayed at the pool with the girls.

She also heard the cell phone on the table ringing constantly and noticed the black Jeep Cherokee in the parking lot with the windows down. Both groups of girls and their mothers left the pool about 4 p.m.

TYLER KEMP, 17 years old, played golf with his friend Evan Sizemore early that afternoon. He returned home about 4 p.m., and then headed to the Foxborough pool in his Jeep so he could take over Ali's shift at 5 p.m. He parked beside Ali's vehicle. He did not see his sister and assumed she would return shortly. He then went into the pump room, took out a skimmer hose and began picking up leaves and debris from the pool.

About 5:15 p.m., when his sister still had not shown up, he became concerned. He called home.

Earlier that day, Roger Kemp had experienced trouble with his

Toyota and dropped it off for repairs.

"The dealership gave me an ugly little car for a loaner," he recalls. "I thought it was humorous. I came home early that day — to show everybody this funny little car."

He arrived home about 5:15 p.m.

"I just walked in the door and the phone was ringing. My wife answered. It was Tyler. He said he couldn't find Ali."

By 5:25 p.m., Roger Kemp was at the pool. He saw Ali's vehicle in the parking lot.

He went quickly into the pool complex, talked briefly with Tyler and headed for the pool area.

He looked in the shallow end. Nothing. He walked to the deep end of the L-shaped pool. Again, nothing. He looked out over the grounds and saw nothing.

Then he walked to the pump room. The doors were open. He hesitated, took a few steps inside and looked around.

The room was cluttered and disorganized. Pool paraphernalia was scattered about. To his left, he noticed a leg sticking out from beneath a tarpaulin.

With no idea what he was about to see, he pulled the tarp away and found a woman face down on the cement floor, one arm at her side and the other underneath her. Clothing was pushed up around her neck.

He turned her over. Her face was covered with hair and the hair was matted with blood. He pulled back the hair. To his horror, Roger Kemp saw that it was Ali.

H E HELD HER HANDS. They were cold. He detected no pulse.

"Her face," he remembers, "was a very bad blue; I saw how savagely she had been assaulted. I talked to her and begged her to come back, I told her to please hang on; help was on the way."

Sarah Reed, a dispatcher with the Leawood Police Department, remembers the call from Roger Kemp at 5:32 p.m. Instantly she "double-toned it," signaling an emergency through the police communication system. She classified it as a J-1 situation, which means a homicide had occurred.

Reed's fellow dispatcher, Lori Sanders, stayed on the phone with Roger Kemp until emergency crews arrived at the pool.

Again and again Ali's father repeated to the dispatcher: "She's not moving; there is blood all over; it looks bad. Ali, please, stay with us. Please, come back!"

About 5:34 p.m. City of Leawood firemen Eric Peterson and Mike Hoffine drove their ambulance out of the fire station at 127th Street and Mission Road with lights and sirens on. Minutes later, they arrived at the Foxborough pool.

Tyler Kemp ran to the corner and frantically waved the ambulance into the parking lot. He hurriedly led the emergency workers to the pump room. There they saw Roger Kemp, holding Ali's hands and urgently talking to her.

The firemen got no response from her. They checked her carotid artery twice, looking for a pulse. There was none.

"Mike Hoffine started doing CPR compressions," Peterson recalls, "and I grabbed our oxygen kit."

Officer Sean Mulcahy, a nine-year veteran of the Leawood Police, was the first policeman to arrive. He found the paramedics dressing Ali's injuries and trying to find a pulse. Around Ali, the floor was covered with blood. He began administering artificial resuscitation.

Hoffine hooked up a defibrillator — one pad above Ali's heart and the other to her side — to administer electrical shock and restore her heart's rhythm. There was no activity.

Then a Johnson County Med-Act crew drove up, carrying more advanced defibrillator equipment and it was hooked to Ali. The county personnel could find no pulse, either.

About 5:45 p.m., Leawood Officer Shawn Farris arrived, found the pump room crowded and ordered Ali moved outside. Paramedics worked on her for a minute and a half more, and then she was moved to the Johnson County Med-Act ambulance and rushed to St. Joseph Medical Center, about four miles north. As they raced to the emergency room, Peterson continued to do CPR compressions.

Meanwhile, Leawood policeman Rodman Lasley arrived at the pool complex. He found emergency personnel near the pool and clubhouse area and a lawn-care trailer in the parking lot along with six or seven squad cars. The victim's car and her father's car were also in the parking lot, along with several other cars.

Lasley's assignment was to control the entrance to the parking area, which he did by parking his squad car next to it and running yellow crime scene tape around the boundaries of the pool complex. As people who were neither police nor emergency personnel left the lot in their cars, he wrote down their names.

"I didn't ask for identification," he explains, "but I did stop each car to ask for the driver's name and phone numbers."

His list contained five names. One of them was Teddy Hoover. His cellphone number: 913-488-1190.

THAT DAY, MAJOR CRAIG HILL, a 35-year police veteran and deputy chief of the Leawood Police, was north of the Kansas City area, giving a presentation about crimes against children and how to make communities safer from sexual predators. Hill's expertise in the field of childhood safety was nationally known. Area government and police personnel attended the lecture. That afternoon, while driving south to Leawood, Hill heard the dispatcher tell of a possible homicide at the Foxborough pool. The major was astonished.

At the same moment, Leawood police detectives Scott Hansen, Joe Langer, John Dickey and Tony Woollen, all veteran investigators, were in mid-town Kansas City, Missouri, working with Kansas City police investigating an auto theft ring. They were called away by word of a possible deceased subject, in their own city. Hansen and Woollen, incredulous, left immediately for the crime scene. Langer and Dickey went directly to St. Joseph's hospital to determine the victim's condition.

SOMETIME BEFORE 6 P.M. Laurel Vine and her mother, both now at home, heard a message on their answering machine from Kate Zitterkoph, a close friend of Laurel and Ali.

Kate, Laurel says, "was crying and kind of screaming so we really couldn't — but my mom said something has happened to Ali." Kate had "already left for the hospital and that I needed to get there." Laurel and her mother headed to the hospital.

Phil Howes tried to call Ali at 6 p.m. to see whether she was ready to go to dinner. Ali's brother Drew answered the call. Phil wondered why Drew was answering Ali's phone.

"Drew asked me if I knew what had happened," Phil explains, "and I said no." The phone went silent as Drew handed it to Kathy Kemp. She told Phil that Ali had been attacked and they were going to the hospital. Phil told his parents about the call and together they, too, went there.

In St. Joseph's emergency room, Ali's friends found paramedics, police, medical personnel and family. There was horror and pain. People seemed almost paralyzed with shock and despair; some were breaking down and crying, some were holding hands and others were talking quietly in small groups. Detective Langer spoke with the Kemps while his colleague, Dickey, stayed in the examination room. Then Dickey came out with the news: Ali Kemp had been pronounced dead at 6:13 p.m.

LATER THAT EVENING, TALKING with a shattered Roger and Kathy Kemp, Detective Langer asked a tough but necessary question: Did their daughter have a problem of any sort with a friend or an acquaintance? The Kemps said Ali had been quite popular and had many friends. The idea of a violent attack by someone she knew seemed out of the question.

Langer chose his next words carefully. It was about 7:30 p.m, only 4½ hours since Ali had been assaulted. Quietly and deliberately, Langer told the Kemps that things were pointing in the direction of a stranger's having committed the crime, and that tracking down the killer would not be easy.

"I told him that he will have to be patient with us," Langer recalls. "We would be in this thing for the long haul — but we are not going to let it die."

2

Benjamin Appleby

*"I went to as many concerts as I could, and drank
as much as I could. I was kind of wild."*
— Benjamin Appleby on his life after his first prison sentence

The town of Stover lies in Ozark country in central Missouri, on one of the primary routes for weekenders and vacation-goers between the Kansas City area and the Lake of the Ozarks.

In the middle 1970s, about 900 people lived there. For many, life was hardscrabble tough. One in five lived on or below the poverty line, and the median household income was $26,000. Many people in Morgan County barely got along, and most did without luxuries.

That was the world Benjamin Allen Appleby entered on June 6, 1975.

His father, Gary Appleby, worked in construction and farming, often as many as 60 hours a week. Like many of their neighbors, the Applebys went from paycheck to paycheck, usually with nothing in between. For a while, the family lived in a rustic house on 160 areas and raised cattle. Benjamin also spent time with his grandparents, who lived down the road. The boy rode on a tractor with his grandfather and pitched in with farm work and construction of a rock garden.

As he grew, Benjamin helped his father with manual labor at excavation sites near their home. The extra money he earned helped pay for a motorbike, which Benjamin took motocross racing on dirt tracks.

In school, says Appleby's sister, "Most of the time he was bored because he knew more than was being taught in class." His grades were not good.

At home things were not good, either. In a small country town, work was scarce. Time and again, money was in short supply. Sometimes, his mother, Joyce Appleby, and his father fought. Sometimes things got physical.

When Benjamin was in middle school, the family moved south to a cottage near Osage Beach in the Lake of the Ozarks resort area. Until the move, mother and father's fights had subsided. In Osage Beach, all hell broke loose. Fights resumed and blows were struck.

"Gary was abusive to me and to the kids," Joyce Appleby said, "both physically. Mainly me — but there were a few times that he got a little carried away with them."

Beset by money problems and emotional problems, the Appleby marriage came apart.

The divorce was acrimonious, and it hit Benjamin hard. The only family he had known collapsed. Years later, psychologists said that the breakup created psychological damage from which he never recovered.

About the same time, Appleby's best friend died in an automobile accident. The two were 13. That loss, too, lingered with Benjamin.

After the divorce, he found himself moving again, first with his father to rural Tonganoxie, Kansas, which is on the western edge of metropolitan Kansas City. Later he also lived on and off with his mother in Independence, Missouri, east of Kansas City, switching back and forth between his parents' homes.

When he reached 15 years of age, Benjamin Appleby had an encounter with the law. On August 8, 1991, Benjamin and a friend, Noah Biddell, left Noah's home in Tonganoxie for an afternoon at the McLouth Threshing Bee. The event, which features old-time, steam-powered farm equipment, is an annual carnival at the fairgrounds in McLouth, Kansas, a small town of about 800 people about 11 miles by road from Tonganoxie.

Evidently, Benjamin was expecting trouble. He carried a stolen .357 Magnum revolver in Noah's car.

Just before midnight that evening, trouble arrived. Tony E. Hubbard, Robert J. Kramer and Dawn L. Mann confronted Noah and Benjamin in the fairgrounds parking lot. Kramer, in particular, was angry with Benjamin; he believed that Benjamin had stolen a valuable gold coin from his parents' home. Benjamin denied it. There was a standoff and some shouting.

While Noah remained in the car, Benjamin got out and confronted all three men. He cocked the revolver and pointed it directly at Tony Hubbard. Kramer tried to grab the weapon, there was a struggle, and the powerful revolver went off. Kramer was struck on the hand, but suffered only slight powder burns and injuries from metal fragments. Police arrived and calmer heads prevailed.

After the matter was sorted out by the Jefferson County Sheriff's Department, Appleby was not charged.

Living as he did at least part of the time with his mother in Independence, Benjamin was enrolled at Truman High School there. At Truman, he excelled in the 152-pound weight class in wrestling; he was a part of the team that won a league championship in 1992. Impressed by his son's ability, Gary Appleby found enough money to send Benjamin to wrestling camp at the University of Oklahoma.

"You weren't going to see him going to college for free or nothing," Noah Bidell remembers, "but he could definitely hold his own on the mat." Benjamin also alternated between fullback and linebacker on the school's football team.

He dropped out of Truman High School in 1992 and never returned. He continued to live a double life, moving back and forth between two homes, one in Tonganoxie and one in Independence. In fact, neither was truly home.

Benjamin was largely out of control. More often than not, as he acknowledged, he "stole beer out of the fridge" and most weekends wound up dead drunk.

A classmate of Benjamin's at Truman High, Cherrie Eckenfels, remembered him as a class clown who could be cruel.

"We had a girl," Eckenfels said, "that had a walker; she was handicapped and she would fall down in the halls sometimes. He would just stand there and laugh at her."

By the time he turned 17, while living at his mother's place in Independence, he found himself for the first time in serious trouble with police.

He and a friend, Adam Champagne, stole a Mercedes owned by Champagne's mother. They ruined the car's transmission. According to Benjamin's mother, Champagne's mother "got very irate, told her son that he was out of the will and all this and that." Trying to set the matter right, "Ben and him decided to get the money for the transmission."

They chose armed robbery.

About 2 a.m. on June 27, 1992, Benjamin, wearing a ski mask and carrying a sawed-off shotgun, made his way into the Winchell's Donut House on 23rd Street in Independence. He jumped over the front counter, pushed an employee, Felipe J. Diaz, against a store wall and demanded money. Diaz emptied the cash register and gave Appleby $70. It was all the store had on hand. Benjamin told the store clerk to lie on his back on the tile floor and taped the clerk's wrists and legs with gray duct tape.

Benjamin then stood up, pointed the shotgun at the head of the terrified clerk and pulled the trigger. There was only a loud click. He ran from the building and pulled off his ski mask. A couple was driving by the store at the time; they stopped, saw the robbery, and later identified Benjamin.

About an hour later, at Town and Country Convenience store on Noland Road near downtown Independence, the two struck again. Benjamin, once more wearing a ski mask and carrying a sawed-off shotgun, confronted Michael J. Evans, the night clerk. Adam Champagne kept a lookout by the front door. Benjamin demanded money from the safe. The clerk told him the safe was timed, but he could give him money from the changer. Evans hurriedly gave Appleby a plastic tube containing two $10 bills and three paper bags with keys to the video games, which normally contained money. Appleby ordered Evans to lie down on the tile floor, pointed the shotgun at his head and pulled the trigger. Again, there was only a loud click. Appleby then said to Champagne, "Let's get out of here."

Two minutes later, at 3:15 a.m., Independence policeman David Steinhauser, who was patrolling the area, heard the dispatcher describe suspects involved in the Winchell's robbery. Almost immediately, he was dispatched to the Town and Country Convenience Store. At Walnut and Lee's Summit Road, a few blocks from the convenience store, Steinhauser saw two white men in a 1972 Chevrolet pick-up truck with license plate Missouri TP7777.

Steinhauser signaled the truck to pull over and ordered both men to remain in the vehicle with their hands up. Benjamin, on the passenger side, bent down as he slowly opened the door. The policeman saw the barrel of a shotgun on the floor, thought he saw Benjamin moving to pick up the weapon, and fired at him. Uninjured, Benjamin fled on foot into the darkness. The driver, Adam Champagne, was taken into custody. Adam was searched and officers found $48, which he said came from Winchell's; he told officers that the person who ran from the scene was Benjamin Appleby. Meanwhile, another policeman searched the area. Soon Benjamin, with his ski mask off, approached him with his hands up and said he was responsible for the robberies. He was taken into custody.

Years later, he told a therapist that the shotgun he carried during the robberies was not loaded.

Adam Champagne was tried as a juvenile and received probation. Benjamin, having confessed to an Independence detective and with other evidence against him, pleaded guilty on March 8, 1993, to the armed robberies.

Before sentencing, Gary Appleby told the Court that his son had been placed in a 30-day treatment program on the recommendation of a psychiatrist and a pretrial release counselor. The court allowed Benjamin to complete the program and on June 21, 1993, barely two weeks after turning 18, he entered prison in Boonville, Missouri. He served almost a year and found it an ugly experience.

"It was pretty rough," Benjamin said. "If you are not a violent person, you're pretty much forced to be a violent person."

After his early release in spring 1994, Appleby's father found work for him at an excavating company in southern Missouri. He also worked in the central Missouri towns of Fulton and Boonville.

"I went to as many concerts as I could," he recalled, "and drank as much as I could. I was kind of wild."

Prison apparently had not made an impression. Only six months after his release, Appleby again crossed the line. In December 1994 he was arrested, charged with and convicted of indecent exposure in Blue Springs, Missouri, on the eastern edge of the Kansas City metropolitan area. He served no time for it.

Thirteen months later, in the early evening of January 20, 1996, in the Westport entertainment district in Kansas City, Dominique Solcher and her friend, Alisa Van Gammeren, both 23, were walking to their car. In disbelief, they saw a man masturbating in an automobile parked nearby. It was Benjamin Appleby. He shouted, "Hey!" and the women, frightened and disgusted, ran to their car and locked the doors. Appleby pulled his car next to theirs on the passenger side, got out and stood, continuing to expose himself. Then he got back into his car. As he drove away, the women took down the number of the Missouri plate, 2Z1121, and called the police.

At police headquarters, the women picked from a spread of photos one of Benjamin Appleby. He was apprehended quickly. In September 1996, because of the incident in Westport and the earlier one in Blue Springs, Appleby was sentenced in Jackson County Circuit Court to 120 days in jail. He told his mother that he had been in a fight with a cab driver.

He was released in late November and placed on probation. Under its terms, he had to complete programs for anger control, chemical dependency and sex-offenders, to refrain from alcohol and to stay out of bars.

In a report to his probation officer, a therapist described Appleby as deeply troubled. Psychologically, he was extremely immature, abused alcohol, had continually caused trouble at school, and did not understand the severity of his own sexual misconduct. He was in a "high risk position to re-offend," the therapist warned, with the real possibility of posing serious physical or sexual harm to others.

The report ended by saying he wanted to "make appropriate changes in his life and his behavior."

On February 12, 1997, he exposed himself to a 17-year-old girl outside Turner High School in Wyandotte County, Kansas. On April 8, a warrant was issued for his arrest, but police could not find him. Appleby, by then 23 and an ex-convict, undoubtedly knew that authorities were looking for him; it would be only a matter of time before he was back in prison. This time the sentence would be much longer.

The easiest way to avoid more trouble, he figured, was to leave town. Before doing so, he obtained a copy of the birth certificate of his childhood friend in central Missouri, the one who died in an auto accident when both were 13. With it he could create an alias using his dead friend's name.

The name: Teddy Hoover.

3

Night of Anguish

*"Her mother and father came in, and upon seeing Ali Kemp in the
exam room, they were just completely devastated....
Perhaps the saddest thing I had ever seen."*
— Dianna Johnson, Leawood police

Just before 7 p.m. on June 18, 2002, Mayor Peggy Dunn
of Leawood entered the large conference room at City Hall
for a meeting of the Finance Committee. It included the city
administrator, the city council and all department heads.

Police Chief Sid Mitchell pulled her aside.

"We went out into the hall outside of the conference room,"
the mayor recalls, "and the chief asked me, 'Don't you know Roger
Kemp?' I said, Yes I did, and I also know Kathy Kemp. Why?

"He told me that Roger had found his daughter murdered at
the Foxborough community pool."

A few minutes later the meeting began. Still stunned, Mayor
Dunn told the council what had happened. The council was
thunderstruck. On that night's agenda were staffing needs and
budgets; now, the discussion promptly focused on a need for more
police.

"We were so astonished," Dunn recalls. "There seemed to be
the feeling that we had somehow left ourselves vulnerable.

"The council's collective thoughts that night led almost to the
feeling that there might be a need for a policeman on every corner,
that this is not going to happen in Leawood again."

DIANNA JOHNSON, a Leawood policewoman for four years,
was a specialist in gathering forensic evidence from victims
of sexual assault, and served as a board member of the Johnson
County Rape Evidence Collection Team.

At 6:19 p.m. on the day Ali Kemp died, she was sent to St. Joseph's Hospital. Arriving 15 minutes later, she was directed to a private examination room near the emergency ward. It contained Ali's body. Detective John Dickey and a nurse were also in the room.

Paramedics already had cut the victim's clothing open during life-saving procedures at the pool. Johnson removed what was left of Ali's clothes. It was obvious that Ali Kemp had been in a brutal physical confrontation.

At 6:47 p.m., Michael Handler, a physician who is the Johnson County deputy coroner, arrived. Wearing surgical gloves, Johnson and Handler began to document the injuries. They did a series of physical examinations using the basic forensics evidence collection kit, which includes swabs and containers for collecting blood and saliva samples. Dickey had a digital camera that Johnson used to take 50 photographs of the victim; a one-line description accompanied each photo. Johnson found the fingers on the victim's left hand were broken, testimony to how terrible the struggle had been.

Working quickly, Johnson and Handler took fingernail and other scrapings. Fingernails were cut halfway back, multiple hair samples were taken from the victim's mouth and back, and leaves and twigs were removed from her hair and back. Other procedures would be completed the next day at the autopsy.

The hospital, Handler recalls, "was somewhat of a chaotic scene."

"The family was pressing to have access to her body and we were sensitive to that."

ABOUT 7 P.M., Leawood Detective Joe Langer talked with Roger and Kathy Kemp in the hallway adjacent to the emergency ward. He knew they wanted to see Ali as soon as possible.

"We will get you into the examination room," he recalls saying, "but I had to ask them, as hard as it will be for them, to not touch her, because we do not want to damage any of the forensic evidence.

"I know that you want to touch her and hug her and we just can't do that right now, and they understood that."

The floor and examination table were covered with blood. Johnson placed a clean white sheet over the victim. She and Detective Dickey did what they could to make Ali and the room as presentable as possible.

"The examination itself seemed painstakingly long," Johnson remembers. "It was so exhaustive and it was so incredibly sad. It was so hard for me to live through.

"Her mother and father came in, and upon seeing Ali Kemp in the exam room, they were just completely devastated, just completely shattered and utterly distraught, just totally beside themselves. I so wished that I could have helped them in some way. Perhaps the saddest thing I had ever seen."

It was after midnight when Johnson delivered evidence bags to the Johnson County Crime Laboratory. Dana Soderholm, a forensic specialist with the lab, received them for analysis.

A T THE FOXBOROUGH POOL, people had gathered outside the yellow tape that sealed off the crime scene. Some were alone and others in small groups. The extent of the horror was not yet known. The day was hot, rumors were running, curiosity was high and the situation was tense.

To add to the confusion, there were roughly 200 asphalt workers nearby, repaving State Line Road. The street was torn up in both directions. Two teams of detectives questioned the workers; all were cleared.

Meanwhile, police tried to reach people who had been at the pool that day. Two lawn-care workers had seen the suspect's truck and given a description; it was probably a 1980s Ford pick-up.

About 8:45 p.m. representatives of the Johnson County Crime Laboratory arrived at the pool and began gathering physical evidence. Over the next hour, Assistant Lab Director Allen Hamm and Deputy Mike Shepard walked through the scene of the crime. Shepard took about 60 photographs.

"Our intent," Hamm recalls, "was to capture the crime scene at its earliest stages before more people had access and things either got walked on or trampled or moved."

At 10:42 p.m. a search warrant arrived, authorizing full access to the area. The pump house was examined by Deputy Dan Rundle with an alternative light source to determine whether body fluids were present. Six areas were tested closely but no semen was found.

A rough sketch of the crime scene was produced, depicting where blood stains and other items of evidence were found. Rundle also collected samples from the pump room floor with sterile cotton swabs, including pool items and supplies.

The crime lab investigators found a triple antibiotic ointment tube on the pump room floor.

"The tube looked out of place," Lab Deputy Lyla Thompson recalled, "because it was just lying on the floor by itself."

It bore reddish-brown stains and its cap was found some distance away.

An opened first aid kit was found. Reddish-brown stains were found on a skimmer pole. All the items were removed from the pump house for further study. Thompson also dusted areas in the room for latent prints. The team of specialists completed its work at the crime scene at 3 a.m. on June 19.

LAUREL VINE KNEW she had critical information: "I told my mom that I thought I had seen someone at the pool when I was there visiting."

That night, Detective Joe Langer talked with her. She told him that she had seen the suspect within a few feet, probably twice.

The first time, she said, the man walked out of the pool area and down the sidewalk. Seeing Laurel in her car, he turned around and went back to the pump room. He came out a second time, waved to her and walked to his truck in the parking lot.

Nothing seemed unusual.

"I presumed he was a maintenance worker. And I just kind of looked around. I saw Ali's stuff there and I just assumed that she had gone to do something really quickly."

Laurel now knew that she, too, could have been assaulted.

She was the only witness, and Langer had to ask her whether she would help create a composite illustration of the suspect. Despite her extreme distress that evening, she said she would try her best.

ROGER AND KATHY KEMP SPENT a few more moments with Ali in the emergency room and then left the hospital. As they left, Joe Langer thought about one of his own daughters, a year younger than the victim and also a student at Kansas State. He could scarcely imagine the emotional ordeal facing Ali's parents. Even if they both lived for a century, would the terrible suffering of this day would ever leave them?

About midnight, Ali's body was transported from St. Joseph's to the pathology department at the University of Kansas Medical Center in Kansas City, Kansas. The autopsy would take place there.

Roger Kemp had almost no sleep for the next few days.

"I spent the night at KU Medical Center," he recalls. "Ali's body was in another room. Two friends stayed up with me all night. The next morning I spoke with the two pathologists scheduled for the autopsy and asked them to do their work well because I would never want to exhume Ali's body once she was interred."

4

The Investigation Begins

*"I wondered, where in God's green earth do we start
and how far do we journey?"*
— Major Craig Hill, Leawood, Kansas, Police Department

Six hours after the slaying of Ali Kemp, Leawood detectives met with Major Craig Hill at police headquarters. With five detectives on staff, the task facing the department was enormous. Few homicides had occurred in Leawood, and those had involved adults connected with other adults — cases involving motives. This homicide was without a motive.

There was nothing to start with. Unlike many other homicides, the victim had no criminal background and no enemies. She was not killed in a drug deal, or during the commission of a crime, or in a domestic argument. Instead, she was simply a woman working at a seemingly safe summer job only a mile from her home. Ali Kemp was an innocent victim.

Hill told Leawood city officials, horrified at what had happened to a young person in their city, that the investigation was going to take resources, a great deal of money and a lot of time.

When a major crime occurs in the Kansas City area, the Metropolitan Area Major Case Squad comes together. It is authorized to cross the multiple city, county and state boundaries covered by the metropolitan area and can act rapidly at the request of any local law-enforcement agency. Wherever it goes, the unit falls under the supervision of the chief administrator in that municipality.

Hill asked the governing board of the Major Case Squad to assemble a team to meet the next day at the Leawood Police

Department. The board approved and directed Kansas City Police Detective Tom Prudden to summon help from across the metropolitan area. Prudden, who would act as press officer for the squad, pulled up his call-out sheet.

By 10:30 a.m. on June 19, the morning after Ali's death, 24 detectives from around the Kansas City area had set up offices in the Leawood Police Department's main building. Major Hill would be in charge of the investigation. Tim Burnette of the police in Merriam, another Johnson County suburban city, would keep track of leads as they developed and assign them to detectives. Joe Langer of Leawood would be the lead detective. Tables, chairs, telephones and computers were in place.

Hill told the group that in his 35 years as a police officer "this was the most brutal, most horrific crime I've ever seen." The difficulties, he said, would be great. The predator was capable of violence. He could be anywhere, and could strike again without warning.

"I wondered," Hill recalls, "Where in God's green earth do we start and how far do we journey?"

After a trip to the crime scene with the detectives, crime lab personnel and the district attorney, Hill took the Major Case Squad detectives to the Kemp home in Leawood.

Roger Kemp remembers the visit well:

"They came from everywhere in the Kansas City metropolitan area. It looked as if some had tears in their eyes, and I knew that I could not ask for anything more. I knew that sooner or later they would find this criminal. It had to happen. It simply had to happen, even if it took 10 years or longer."

After that, Hill contacted Roger Kemp every day about the squad's progress.

The first goal for the squad was to find anyone who knew Ali or who had been at the pool on the day she died. Detectives went to Ali's bedroom and looked through her belongings. Because she had been away at college in the spring, they searched through school papers, notebooks, everything — looking for any lead. Her computer was taken to police headquarters, but nothing unusual was found.

Police also talked to her boyfriend, Phil Howes, to her brothers and to her parents. They checked their DNA and apologized for having to check their individual reports.

"Through all of this," Roger Kemp recalls, "I knew they were doing their job and it was obvious that they were doing it thoroughly."

In many places in the United States, homicides have become almost commonplace. In most cases, there is not a lot for the police press officer to do, because there is not a lot of public interest. In the Ali Kemp case, Tom Prudden remembers, police could have used several press officers.

"The media was at our door non-stop every day, every night, wanting interviews, wanting to find out what was happening," he said. "The case generated more media interest than any case I have ever seen."

Leads from the Kansas City Crime Commission's TIPS Hotline started coming in. Police phones rang all day, every day. Reporters were constantly at police headquarters and at the pool, and sometimes they followed investigators who were following up on leads.

Few cases in Kansas City had ever caused such public response. Most homicides generated about 150 leads through the course of an investigation. In the Ali Kemp case, more than 1,500 leads came in early. The total later climbed to 3,000 and finally surpassed 7,000 — an incredible public reaction to the mortal tragedy of a single individual. More calls came in to the Kansas City Crime Commission than in any case in its history. Many called to express their outrage and sympathy. Many said they couldn't believe what had happened. Many said, "I hope to God you get the guy."

THE AUTOPSY OF ALI KEMP took place at the University of Kansas Medical Center in Kansas City, Kansas, on the day after she died. The deputy county coroner, Michael Handler, was the pathologist. Leawood Detective Tony Woollen was there to photograph the victim's injuries and to receive evidence provided by Handler. He took 62 photos. Under Johnson County policy for homicide autopsies, an assistant district attorney, Steve Howe, was also present.

On pre-drawn diagrams, Handler documented severe blunt-force injuries. Among them were black eyes, blows to her mouth, bruises on the side of her head, bruises on her left shoulder and both arms, lacerations to the back of her head, bruises on her elbows and pelvis, bruises on her legs, both knees and one foot. Injuries were inflicted within a brief time. There was evidence of a ferocious struggle; death was caused by multiple blunt-force injuries and strangulation.

At the end of the procedure, blood samples in tubes were turned over to Detective Woollen. He placed them in a clear plastic evidence bag, sealed it with evidence tape, initialed the tape and took the samples to police headquarters. Woollen listed the samples with other evidence files, filled out a delivery slip and delivered them to the Johnson County crime lab. Dana Soderholm at the lab received the autopsy evidence bag from Detective Woollen at 4:19 p.m. on June 19. She applied the case number — 02 3398 — and the date, June 19, 2002.

Soderholm conducted a DNA analysis on items found at the crime scene. She found dark reddish-brown stains on each piece of clothing, as well as on the ointment tube and cap that investigators discovered on the floor of the pump room.

Nuclear DNA testing is commonly used throughout the country. In the procedure, scientists look at chromosomes, the rod-shaped structures found in the nucleus of each human cell. The objective is to identify and compile 13 locations in the genetic material. Scientists can then tell the blood of one person from the blood of another. The process provides data with a high degree of certainty.

The chemist ascertained the genetic profile of the victim, Ali Kemp, from the blood stains on the evidence. She also found the blood of an unknown Caucasian male.

His DNA profile was entered into the FBI Laboratory's CODIS System, a computerized index that enables federal, state and local crime labs to exchange DNA information electronically.

The objective was to find the man whose DNA matched the sample.

L AUREL VINE'S SIGHTING of the man leaving the pool was critical. Investigators needed to know what he looked like, and a composite illustration would be crucial.

Lee Hammond, an expert police composite illustrator, volunteered her services. On June 20 at 4:30 p.m., barely 48 hours after the assault on Ali Kemp, Hammond went to work in the Leawood Police conference room with Laurel Vine.

"She was severely traumatized," Hammond says. "I did not allow police officers in the room while we worked. I did not allow tape recorders or video equipment or anything in that room. It was just Laurel and me, one on one. I made sure it was quiet. They disconnected the phones in that room."

The process would take five hours.

Using various physical and mental relaxation techniques, among them breathing techniques and visualization, Hammond was able to move Laurel gradually to a state of mind where she did not focus on the horror or the sadness of Ali's death, but on what she had seen that day.

Eventually, Laurel recaptured the image of the man she had seen at the pool. He was a white male, probably 5 feet 10 inches to 6 feet tall, with a heavy build. He had short brown hair and was wearing something like a blue jumpsuit.

His vehicle, she recalled, was an older model pickup truck — perhaps a Ford — that was light blue or beige. Her memory of it squared with the description given by lawn-care workers.

The result was a composite illustration that police used in their investigation. Helping create it required an enormous act of physical courage, for Laurel Vine was the only person who had seen the assailant. Police knew he could strike again.

O N THE NIGHT OF JUNE 20, HUNDREDS of friends, neighbors and classmates of Ali Kemp and her family walked down Leawood city sidewalks and spilled into the street as they gathered for a vigil at the entrance to the Foxborough pool. For those who knew her and even for those who did not, it was a time of emotion and prayer. At a makeshift shrine, they left flowers, cards, posters, a photo montage of Ali Kemp and Phil Howes together, a Kansas State University T-shirt signed with messages and stuffed animals.

Two days later, a Saturday, at 1 o'clock in the afternoon, more than 1,200 persons packed the United Methodist Church of the Resurrection in Leawood. Ali's mother and dad, her brothers and Phil Howes sat close to Ali Kemp's closed wooden casket, which was covered with white, pink, blue and yellow flowers. Many in attendance carried memorial ribbons in lavender and white, Ali's favorite colors.

The service celebrated her life as full of promise and noted its painful end. Ali was remembered as a happy, talented person with many friends. As the lights dimmed in the large church, a video chronicled her life from childhood to adulthood.

"There is a terrible, evil thing that has happened," Reverend Adam Hamilton said. "It's left a huge hole in our lives. But evil does not and cannot and should not be the final word. There is goodness; Ali showed you that."

She was buried in a landscaped area near a small pond in Mount Moriah Cemetery in southern Kansas City, Missouri. On the day of her funeral, crowds of people lined the sidewalks and narrow roads leading to the site. Hundreds stood quietly on the grounds nearby and listened. When it ended, the crowds departed slowly. Roger Kemp was the last person to leave after he had lowered his daughter's casket to the earth.

From a small shed across a pond at the cemetery, police video cameras taped the graveside service. Police and Roger Kemp would study the video, searching for a possible suspect who might have shown up that day.

BY JUNE 27, INVESTIGATORS had received details of the autopsy. They learned the true extent of Ali's injuries, and that her death was caused by strangulation.

The full autopsy report was not released, but the public was told that there had been a considerable struggle in the pump room and that Ali had suffered severe blunt-force injuries. Their best lead, detectives said, concerned a man seen at the pool on June 18, the last time Ali Kemp was seen alive. If this was the man Laurel Vine had seen, he might show scratches and bruises or other signs of a struggle, they commented. Tom Prudden, the Major Case Squad spokesman, told reporters that police wanted to talk to him.

"He had no apparent reason to be there," Prudden said. "He was there just a short time, and he was there around the last time that she was seen alive."

Metro Area Major Case Squad detectives worked at a furious pace. In addition to following up leads, they tracked down men who had been convicted of sex crimes and recently released from prison. Their work was tedious and time-consuming, and made even more difficult by the sense of horror and the publicity surrounding the case.

Investigators often drove to a suspect's workplace or home or both, and then interviewed him to determine whether he had access to a pickup that matched the suspect's truck. Investigators often asked permission to take DNA samples.

Leawood Detective Ron Hulsey found more than three hundred 1980 and 1981 Ford pickup trucks registered in the Kansas City metropolitan area.

On June 28, the Major Case Squad made public the composite of the man seen by Laurel Vine at the Leawood pool. By the next day, police had the names of more than a hundred men who looked something like him, including a man at a Leawood coffee shop, a man at a Johnson County shopping center, men at a car dealer's showroom in nearby Shawnee, Kansas, a man boarding a plane at Kansas City International Airport and another man digging ditches along the highway south of Olathe, Kansas. Someone reported a man at an Olathe swimming pool.

Others reported seeing trucks similar to the suspect's as far away as St. Joseph and Springfield, Missouri, and Topeka, Kansas.

None of those early leads panned out.

On June 30, the authorization for the Major Case Squad ended. The 24 detectives who gathered to help the Leawood police had investigated more than 800 leads and worked about 2,700 hours. DNA samples were taken from about a dozen men who resembled the suspect.

The Leawood police were grateful for the help.

"It helped to cover an enormous amount of ground to help us eliminate a lot of folks," said Leawood Detective Sergeant Hansen, who would now lead the investigation. Five Leawood detectives were assigned to the case full-time.

Meanwhile, Leawood police sent details of the crime to the FBI's Violent Criminal Apprehension database — a program that helps police across the country link homicides appearing to be random, sexually oriented or part of a series of crimes.

Their work had only just begun.

5

America's Most Wanted

*"There are two ways of dealing with the tragedy of a murdered child.
You can give up or you can fight back."*
— John Walsh, "America's Most Wanted"

In summer 2002 the Fox television series, "America's Most
Wanted: America Fights Back," was beginning its 14th season as
one of the network's longest-running and most successful crime
programs. Audiences of seven to eight million watched every
week, and it was the most widely viewed program in its time slot on
Saturday nights for years. Using fast-paced production techniques
and solid journalism, "America's Most Wanted" targeted dangerous
fugitives anywhere in America; it pursued the criminals profiled on
air until they were caught.

John Walsh, host of the series, experienced tragedy in his
own life, He is the father of Adam Walsh, who was kidnapped
and murdered in 1981. His son's death, the elder Walsh recalls,
"knocked me right on the floor. It felt like somebody took a huge
wooden cross and shoved it into the wall of my chest."

The sadness was overpowering for Walsh and his wife, Reve
Walsh, and as the months went by their pain grew worse.

Walsh watched his wife suffer: "It was like seeing someone
tortured slowly…slowly…and then watching them let out a last sigh
and die."

Somehow, at some point, amidst the emotional wreckage, the
couple turned their personal anguish into public service. They
founded the Adam Walsh Outreach Center for Missing Children.

"If we had not gone on to do what we ultimately did," Walsh
says, "we would have remained as we were: two grief-stricken, hand-
wringing parents whom other people looked at and felt sorry

for. But what we both came to believe was that you are given an opportunity to change, then how can you not at least try?"

They learned firsthand how little help existed anywhere for parents in their situation — searching for justice and facing emotional devastation.

Millions now view Walsh as a leader in the pursuit of justice. Walsh was instrumental in the passage of the federal Missing Children's Act and the founding of the National Center for Missing & Exploited Children. The "America's Most Wanted" series — in which citizens work with authorities to solve crimes — has changed the lives of thousands of crime victims.

Walsh has been honored for his pioneering work in investigative television by four American presidents. He has been named Man of the Year by the FBI and the U.S. Marshals.

The television series, with Walsh as the host since the beginning, has helped police and other investigators find and catch more than 800 fugitives. Because of it, the FBI has removed the names of 13 criminals from its Most Wanted list, and has made it possible over the years for 30 missing children to be returned to their families. Within the last year, calls to the "America's Most Wanted" Hotline surpassed one million.

John Walsh sees his work as a tribute to his fallen son, Adam. The cases in which children and young people are the victims are the ones in which he is most deeply involved.

Major Craig Hill of Leawood had known John Walsh since 1982 and worked with him at the National Crime Prevention Coalition and the National Center for Missing & Exploited Children in Washington. Hill and six other Kansas City-area officers founded the Lost Child Network after Hill had worked on a case involving the abduction and attempted homicide of a 10-year-old girl. The Lost Child Network, a non-profit organization composed of police officers, merged, after 15 years in existence, with the National Center for Missing & Exploited Children.

The death of Ali Kemp, Hill knew, needed national attention and right away. On June 20, he telephoned John Walsh and outlined the events of June 18. Deeply moved, John Walsh acted immediately. He called the executive producer of "America's Most Wanted," Lance Heflin, and began describing the Ali Kemp homicide. Heflin, all business, stopped Walsh almost in mid-sentence.

"All right," Heflin said. "Lemme get on it. Talk to you later." Heflin didn't say goodbye, he never did. The phone went "click."

By the first of July, less than two weeks after Ali's death, Major Hill contacted Roger Kemp to tell him that "America's Most Wanted" would change its production schedule and come to Kansas City immediately.

Later that afternoon, the producer of the CBS program "48 Hours," hosted for years by Dan Rather, called Leawood police and said that he, too, wanted to do a feature on the Ali Kemp homicide.

"'48 Hours' had one foot on the plane," Roger Kemp remembers, "and they were ready to come out from New York and do a story on the crime against Ali. I knew that the enormous exposure could be important to the investigation."

However, "48 Hours" wanted the story on an exclusive basis and "America's Most Wanted" did not.

"I made the decision to go with John Walsh's program," Roger Kemp says. "Although I had respect for Dan Rather, and even though the show would reach millions, I did not like the exclusive aspect of '48 Hours.' I knew also that millions of viewers, including police officers and investigators in every jurisdiction and even prison inmates all across the country, watched 'America's Most Wanted' every week."

The public is inundated with crime news. The mission of "America's Most Wanted" was to get viewers to focus on a single crime, one crime at a time. The show would ask millions of viewers to help solve the case; viewers would be able to anonymously call the "America's Most Wanted" Hotline and report the identity and possible location of anyone suspected in this crime.

Events moved quickly. The search for the killer of Ali Kemp went to the top of the "America's Most Wanted" list. The program's

15-member crew, based in Washington, arrived in Kansas City on July 9 and spent most of the day at the Foxborough community pool, which had been closed since Ali's death.

Beforehand, the crew taped an interview with Roger and Kathy Kemp at their home. Roger Kemp recalled what came next:

"Phil Howes and I met John Walsh at the Leawood pool. Squad cars were there, in the streets around the pool and in the parking lot. Traffic in the neighborhood was completely shut down.

"Police officers and investigators, AMW people and some news reporters were there. It was very, very tense. Emotionally, Phil and I and my wife and Ali's brothers and friends had just about hit bottom. It was a tough day.

"I remember two very large vehicles in that crowded pool parking lot that morning. One was for the production equipment and the other was John Walsh's motor home. Three bodyguards accompanied John Walsh and I was amazed that AMW provided bodyguards for Phil and me during the taping. It was explained to us that the assailant might still be out there and he might target us."

Both men talked with Walsh before taping began. Walsh says he tried to be honest.

"Time does make it easier," Walsh recalls telling Roger Kemp, "but, as painful as it was for me to say, Roger and Kathy will always be the parents of a murdered child. We had some private time talking about how he is going to survive and how his wife is going to survive. There were two beautiful boys that must have been hurting terribly.

"I said that you have to battle to keep your sanity and you have to battle to go to work. I told him that the wound will close, but it will not heal; but you will not forget. Before long, you will know that the empty place in your heart will, in many ways, predict what the rest of your life will be like. I told Roger that I have only found two solutions. The first is, try to remember the good times, the 19 years you and your family had with her. The second: try to be of service to others so that they will not have the pain that you have had."

The horror of Ali's death, Walsh said, was not God's plan, "not the work of God to test them as Job was tested."

The Kemps, he knew, must somehow "live with the fact that their child was not only taken from them, but that she suffered terribly in the hands of a brutal madman in her last hour." He said they must somehow, in some way, not dwell on the savage nature of the assault because thinking about it "will take you to the deepest, darkest part of your soul."

"The Kemps were way ahead of me," Walsh recalls. "They were fighting through the pain and already planning to help others and I knew that would be very significant for them and for others."

Taping the show that morning could not have been more difficult. The day was hot and humid and things were noisy. Asphalt crews were working close to the pool and trucks and construction vehicles constantly passed by. The crime scene was small and crowded; the production, with repeated interruptions by passing vehicles, took the morning and part of the afternoon.

Intros, promos and segues were taped in front of the pump house where Ali was slain.

"Good evening," Walsh said, facing the camera, and speaking in powerful, measured tones. "It's the middle of summer, and this pool in the suburbs of Kansas City should be crowded and full of splashing and laughter. Instead, it is closed, and this pool house behind me was the scene of a shocking murder." Walsh pointed to the pump room.

"This story is absolutely heartbreaking," Walsh continued. "It has not only broken the hearts of Ali's family, but it has also broken the hearts of everyone here in Leawood, Kansas. We've got to work together to catch this coward tonight."

As Walsh spoke, the camera focused first on him and then on the pump room. Viewers saw a full-frame photograph of Ali Kemp, the "America's Most Wanted" toll-free number and the announcement of a $50,000 reward for the tip that would lead to the killer of Ali Kemp.

The taping took place 21 days after the murder, but it seemed to many who were there that the horror had occurred only a few minutes before, as if it was happening all over again.

"Now we take the case from Leawood, Kansas, nationwide,"

Walsh said. "My hopes are that somebody is going to say, I know who that creep is, and make that call."

"AMERICA'S MOST WANTED" headquarters, known as the Crime Center, were in the lower level of a small building in downtown Washington, D.C. A fulltime staff of about 40 kept the operation open and staffed seven days a week; most days brought periods of great activity.

Under the show's policy, calls to the hotline are not answered by police, and are transferred to police only with the caller's permission.

About one-fourth of captures made after an "America's Most Wanted" program occur within the first 24 hours. A smaller number occur in the second 24 hours. On the third day, calls diminish and hope for an early capture usually fades. In some instances, captures have been made after a fourth or even fifth showing

The Ali Kemp segment was scheduled to go on the air August 3. Beforehand, the program's hotline chief, Sharon Greene, met with her staff of 24 operators. Together, they watched the show in advance and reviewed case sheets to become acquainted with the slaying. Greene listed the clues that would be given that night and those that would not. She reminded the operators how calls were to be screened, how tip sheets would be distributed and what information authorities would need.

Before ending each call, operators were instructed to ask, "May we give your name and number to a law enforcement agent, should they wish to call you for more information?" Typically, about 90 percent of callers agree to do so. Operators are also asked to characterize the caller. Was the caller nervous or frightened? Did the caller seem sincere? The information obtained on each call is confidential and may be used for law-enforcement purposes only.

When a caller asks to talk to an investigator, the operator raises his or her hand, signaling a high-priority call. With the caller's permission, the phone is given to a law enforcement investigator.

That night the slaying of Ali Kemp was the lead story on "America's Most Wanted." An estimated 7.4 million people watched. As soon as it was done, the Crime Center phones were inundated and continued that way for hours. The 24 operators, with 48 incoming lines and working non-stop, barely managed to keep up. The calls amounted to the highest number ever from the airing of a single episode.

Leawood Detective Joe Langer, who was standing by, remembers what happened:

"The phones just erupted. I know it broke all records. The calls started coming in at 9 on the East Coast and never stopped."

"I ran back and forth taking the more serious calls, the Level One Calls, all evening until after midnight, when the calls from the West Coast were finished. It was a very, very fast pace all evening, with no breaks in the action.

"Operators screened the calls very carefully. They were exceedingly skillful. The calls they knew lacked content for followup were not given to me. As an example, a caller might say, 'Yeah, I saw him at a bus stop in Milwaukee two months ago,' followed by a hang up, and no more information. The operator would take that call, fill out a tip sheet, but not pass it on to me.

"On the other hand, the more serious calls with more details were given to me. For example, a typical caller came on the line and said, 'You know, my daughter's boyfriend looks exactly like that guy whose picture you had on TV tonight. I know he's been gone all spring and most of the summer and he said he was in Kansas City in June. Her boyfriend really does look like that picture on TV and he has a truck like that one too. You might want to talk to him. He might be the guy you're looking for.' In this situation, the operator raised her hand and I then took the call to get as much information as possible and we started our normal followup process the next week in Leawood.

Of the 248 calls received that night at the Crime Center in Washington, about three-fourths came from Kansas and Missouri.

That same night, 100 more calls went directly to the Leawood Police Department or to the Kansas City Crime Commission's TIPS Hotline, where three extra policemen were on duty.

The next day, Joe Langer reviewed the leads in his Washington hotel room, sorting them by state and by priority.

Upon his return to Leawood, the city's detectives met at

Leawood Police headquarters with special agents of the FBI, the Kansas Bureau of Investigation, detectives from Johnson County and adjacent Miami County and the Johnson County Sheriff's Department.

Again, leads were sorted by location and priority and the agencies went to work.

6

New England and Back

"I carry a lot of things around with me in my head."
— Benjamin Appleby

On February 14, 1997, Benjamin Appleby arrived in Connecticut, a place he had never been. At the bus station in Waterbury he was picked up by Tammy Wyatt, a woman he had never met – except on the Internet. In their communications, he had identified himself to her only as "Ben."

With little cash and only a few clothes, he had traveled far from home to avoid being arrested for incidents of indecent exposure. As a cover, he had adopted the name of his best friend from childhood. That's why he carried a copy of the birth certificate of Teddy L. Hoover. He told Wyatt that Hoover was his real name, and that "Ben" was a nickname his family had given him because he looked like an uncle named Ben.

He and Wyatt headed for her apartment in Northville, where he moved in and began a relationship that was doomed from the start. On arriving, he accused Wyatt of deceiving him by sending him a picture of a friend instead of herself.

Nevertheless, Appleby had no intention of moving out. He also showed he was in no hurry to find work. He drank every night. When he was drunk, Wyatt recalled, "it seemed like he hated me."

About three months after his arrival in Connecticut, the two were "play-fighting, joking around," in Wyatt's apartment. They stood, facing each other. Appleby started a game by pushing her. She pushed him back. Then she pushed him in the shoulder and he pushed her back. Appleby pushed her head away. She slapped him in the lower back.

Appleby then lightly slapped her across the face with his open hand. She asked him why he did that and then lightly slapped him back. Appleby slapped her hard in the face and Wyatt, stunned, tried to slap him back, but Appleby grabbed her hand and broke four of her fingernails.

Later, things calmed down and Appleby apologized.

Appleby spent much of his time in the apartment's living room, playing the stereo with the volume turned way up. Worried about her neighbors, Wyatt asked him to turn the music down, but Appleby evidently was not going to be ordered around. He screamed at Wyatt and called her a Nazi. She lightly slapped Appleby on the back of his head. Infuriated, he grabbed the back of her shirt and pushed her into the dining room table where she banged her face and fell to the floor. If she ever did that again, Appleby told her, he would kill her.

Again, things cooled off.

A week later, the couple went to a party in Newton, Connecticut. Evidently there was a great deal of drinking and Appleby got into a fight. Punches were thrown, followed by pushing, shoving and shouting. Outraged, the host told Wyatt and Appleby to leave. Because Appleby was drunk, Wyatt drove the car back to their apartment in Northville. Appleby disappeared into the bathroom.

After a while, the bathroom door opened and Appleby slowly crawled out on his hands and knees, approached Wyatt and asked her whether she knew how to choke someone. She said no. Appleby stood up and took hold of her neck and squeezed tightly and told her to take hold of his neck and tighten her grip. He said they could kill each other and "nobody would know how or why." Appleby stopped, laughed at her and walked into the kitchen.

Later, Appleby told her his real name. She asked him why he had used an alias, and Appleby replied that after a traffic accident in Kansas City he had beaten severely a 17-year-old black youth — perhaps had even killed him, but he wasn't sure. If Wyatt told anyone, he said, he would kill her.

In June 1997, Appleby moved out.

By leaving the Kansas City area, Appleby had violated his probation order. He had neglected to report to his probation officer. Also he was wanted for exposing himself at Turner High School. On August 1, 1997, his parole was suspended and a warrant issued for his arrest for probation violation.

Now, far away in New England, Appleby continued the pattern.

Just after noon on August 27, a 15-year-old girl at Nonnewaug High School in Woodbury, Connecticut, was walking to the school's administration building. She noticed a small white truck facing the wrong way on the circle drive in front of the school. Inside sat Benjamin Appleby.

He called to the teenager, asking for directions. As she approached the truck to help, she could see inside. Appleby's pants were unzipped and she could see his genitals. She ran inside the administration building and told school officials. The principal contacted police and the victim's mother rushed to the school.

Woodbury policemen Terrance Langin and R.J. Binkowski went to the school and interviewed the victim in the principal's office with her mother present. The girl, although upset and disgusted, was able to describe in general terms the man in the truck, and the officers developed a composite illustration. It provided only a vague depiction of Appleby.

The description was transmitted to nearby police departments and squad cars scoured the area but, whether by cunning or luck, Appleby got away.

In November 1997, Appleby exposed himself again in separate incidents, this time in nearby New Milford.

In the first, Appleby was driving by New Milford High School when he saw two girls standing on a sidewalk. He waved to them and stopped near where they were standing. His pants were down. The girls ran inside and he drove away.

Later, Appleby recalled the incident this way:

"The girls looked over and started to walk away. I opened the truck door and I don't think I said anything. I didn't get out but they looked over because I opened my door. The girls could see what I was doing and they called me an "a_____.""

They ran to the school building. Appleby left and drove to a local fast-food restaurant.

"I went into the bathroom at McDonald's and looked in the mirror and I couldn't really look at myself."

The next episode took place near the top of the New Milford Green, where he saw a young girl walking up the hill toward the high school. With his pants down, he opened the door of the vehicle. Like the others, the girl ran to the school building.

B Y THE END OF HIS FIRST YEAR IN CONNECTICUT, Appleby was occasionally going alone to the Marbledale Pub, a restaurant and bar on the New Milford Turnpike close to New Preston.

There by chance, Appleby met Jim Dobson, owner of Dobson Pools, a pool contractor in New Milford. After the two became acquainted, Dobson sent odd jobs Appleby's way. Among them were repairing and renovating swimming pools, which Appleby did in exchange for rent at a small cottage behind Dobson's business.

There, too, he met Lara Barr, a bartender. He told her his name was Teddy Hoover. The two went out to eat in December 1997, their first date, and although Barr did not care for him at first she later said, "It didn't take me long to fall in love."

A few months later, Appleby told Lara his real name. He said he had been in trouble with the law, but only for urinating in public. He made no mention of the indecent exposure incidents, or the robberies in Independence. Nothing Lara Barr heard changed the way she felt about him.

Then came still another episode. On February 3, 1998, Appleby stopped once again at New Milford High School.

"It was almost," he later wrote, "as if I wanted to get caught."

At 4:30 p.m. that day, he saw a girl drive into the school's lower faculty parking lot, get out of her car and walk toward the school. There was a basketball game at the school that day.

Appleby, still sitting in his car, rolled down the driver's window and yelled in her direction: "Hey! Who you guys playing tonight?" The girl, a cheerleader, responded, "Immaculate." Appleby said, "What?" She took a step closer and saw the door of his car open. The driver was wearing only a brown T-shirt and no pants.

"I turned to run away," she recalled, "and then turned back around to get a plate number. He was still sitting there so I just kept running."

She quickly made her way to the principal's office.

New Milford police put the pieces of evidence together and identified a suspect. Later that week, they found his vehicle — a 1985 Jeep — outside the Marbledale Pub. They waited in the parking lot until he came out, accompanied by Lara Barr. Officers asked him if he would come to the station to provide information about a stolen tank of gas. This confused Lara Barr, and she later said, "He acted just as confused as I was about what was going on."

Still using the alias Teddy Hoover, on February 16 he confessed to the stunning series of incidents.

He was lonely, he told Detective David Shortt of the New Milford Police, and Connecticut was cold and expensive.

"I get depressed," he said, "and I feel like I don't belong and somehow I end up driving around with my pants down. I'm not trying to hurt anyone and I don't want the girls to get in the car with me. I can't understand the whole thing; it is like I am two different people. I know I need professional help."

He mentioned severe problems in his childhood: "I carry a lot of things around with me in my head. My dad was kind of mean and my mom was trapped. It was very hard."

Lying, he said he had never been involved in sexual misconduct until he moved to Connecticut. He also continued to lie about his name. Because of that, Connecticut police did not connect Teddy Hoover with the Benjamin Appleby who was guilty on multiple counts of indecent exposure in the Kansas City area.

Although he signed a confession admitting to the incidents in Connecticut, he was not arrested and was released within an hour. According to the New Milford Police, parts of his confession conflicted with statements by the victims. As a result, they believed that they did not have probable cause to charge him. Later, the state's attorney for that part of Connecticut, John Connelly, said, "I don't know why they didn't charge him right there."

Lara Barr apparently waited at police headquarters while he was being interviewed. When he came out of the interrogation room, she said, he was visibly upset, as if he had been crying.

Eight days after the confession — even though no charges had been filed by New Milford officials — Detective Shortt contacted officer Langin in Woodbury. He told Langin about the confession, which included the incident at Nonnewaug High School in Woodbury. On April 15, 1998, a warrant was issued for the arrest of the man known as Teddy Hoover for public indecency and disorderly conduct.

Beginning May 12, New Milford and Connecticut State Police began trying to find him. First they went to the place he had rented at Dobson Pools in New Milford, where the owner told them that their suspect had moved out. He mentioned Lara Barr's home in Washington, Connecticut, but police did not find him there, either. They tried Barr's mother, Ina E. Barr-Jalbert, who lived in New Preston. She told him that the accused had stayed there several nights with her daughter, but had moved the previous week. She did not know where he was now living.

Again in September, acting on new and, as it turned out, incorrect information, police went to Barr-Jalbert's home in vain. After that, the arrest warrant for Teddy Hoover was filed as a fugitive case.

By then, he was back in the Midwest.

IN LATE SPRING 1998, Appleby had told Lara Barr that he wanted to return to the Kansas City area and wanted her to go with him.

"There was something about him," she said. "I didn't have to think twice."

The couple headed for Kansas City, Kansas, where they rented the first floor of a three-story house on a narrow, dead-end road at 49 South 64th Street. Their new home was about a block from where Appleby's father lived.

Neighbors, who knew him as Teddy Hoover, found him to be a rude and vulgar man who hosted loud parties.

"There was something creepy about him," a former neighbor recalled. "My husband and I were both creeped out by him; he made us nervous."

Yet his friends remembered him and Barr as a fun couple to be around on weekends.

"He was one of those guys," said Jesse Eldringhoff, who with his wife, Jennifer, often spent time with Appleby and Barr. "If you said he was coming over, you knew you were going to laugh until the sun came up."

Maintaining the alias of Teddy L. Hoover, Appleby found a job with a local pool and spa company. In late summer 2001 he opened his own pool-maintenance company under the name Hoover Pool Services. It operated from his residence in Kansas City, Kansas. His work often took him to some of Kansas City's wealthiest suburbs, including Leawood.

Appleby did business with suppliers of pool-cleaning equipment and chemicals in suburban Johnson County. Trey Bruce, an employee with Superior Pool Products in Lenexa, said the man who called himself Teddy Hoover was a regular customer who opened an account in March 2001. Employees of nearby Great Plains Supply, with whom Appleby also opened a business account, said he "seemed like a happy-go-lucky guy."

In December 2001, over dinner at Pierpont's restaurant in Kansas City's refurbished Union Station, Appleby proposed marriage and Barr accepted. As she remembers, "He started crying before he took the ring out." The happy couple finished the night at Kansas City's Westin Crown Center hotel facing the Mayor's Christmas tree on the square below.

A few days afterward, on December 17, Appleby was driving along State Line Road between Leawood and Kansas City, Missouri. At 4:15 p.m., his maroon Ford pickup truck collided with a vehicle operated by a drunken driver, who was taken into custody. Leawood policewoman Dianna Johnson took the names of both drivers. Appleby gave his name as Teddy L. Hoover II, and his business number, which was that of his cell phone, as (913) 448-1190.

One day, the record of that incident would play a part in solving the mystery of Ali Kemp's slaying. Until then, investigators would face years of dead ends, wrong turns and misleading tips.

7

The Long Search

"At any one time, we probably had enough leads
and tips for 25 detectives. "
— Leawood Detective Joe Langer

As June 2002 turned into July, Detective Sergeant Scott Hansen of the Leawood Police had his hands full. With the disbanding of the Metropolitan Area Major Case Squad, the number of investigators into Ali Kemp's murder dropped from 25 to six. It would be the largest investigation the Leawood department had ever handled, and for sheer size, use of manpower and number of leads and tips, it would be virtually unmatched in Kansas City area history. The Johnson County Sheriff's Department lent two investigators for a while. Two Leawood patrolmen were assigned to help. Hansen was in day-to-day charge.

On June 30, he met Roger Kemp for the first time.

"I reassured him," Hansen recalls, "that we were going to keep working the investigation aggressively to find the person who killed his daughter and bring that person to justice."

The mood at police headquarters was urgent. Hansen gathered with detectives and unit secretary Alison Wacker early every morning. They reviewed developments from the day before and discussed priorities for the day ahead. Because of the continuing avalanche of leads, the detectives established a computer database devoted to the Ali Kemp investigation. The idea, Hansen said, was to "eliminate the possibility that an investigator might make six or seven calls on the same guy, when one call would do. It also helped us keep track of what information we had on each guy."

Police had no idea who the assailant was or what his intent had been. Had he focused on one female victim that day? Had he been watching women and girls at the pool? If so, had he done it for days before, or the day before, or only on June 18?

Investigators were intrigued by a report that a man was seen the day before Ali's slaying, lurking with a camera or binoculars in the shrubs near the south side of the pool. He was described as a white male, 20 to 40 years old, wearing a dark shirt and a baseball cap on backward. Witnesses said he appeared to be taking photographs of two women sitting in lounge chairs inside the pool area. He was seen briefly about 12:30 p.m. and then disappeared. Whoever he was, this person haunted investigators.

Was he the same person who assaulted Ali Kemp the next day? If not, who was he? Were two assailants involved? If so, why did Laurel Vine see only one person leaving the pump room the day of Ali's death, and why did the unknown DNA that had been gathered come from only one donor?

Early on, the possibility that the killing might be the work of a serial killer occurred.

"If it was a guy who was a stranger or a serial killer," Detective Joe Langer said, "we know they go in to an area, they stay maybe for a short time, they kill a victim and then move and nobody will ever know."

Two lawn-care workers who were at the pool the day of Ali's death had seen a tan pickup truck, Hansen said. It entered the parking lot and circled the area three or four times. In the middle of the afternoon, they saw it leave.

Detectives decided that it had to be the same truck that Laurel Vine saw in the pool parking lot about the time of the murder.

SIXTEEN DAYS AFTER THE HOMICIDE, on Independence Day 2002, Benjamin Appleby and Lara Barr attended an outdoor Fourth of July party given by their friends Jennifer and Jesse Eldringhoff.

"I just remember him being the one that was shooting people with bottle rockets and blowing up stuff in the driveway and being rowdy," Jennifer recalled. Appleby was popular with the men in their crowd, but many of the women were of a different opinion. He could be coarse, and he often made sexual comments and off-

The infant Alexandra
Kemp. She was the
first child of Roger
and Kathy Kemp.

Sitting for her portrait.

Growing up, soccer was
a favorite pastime.

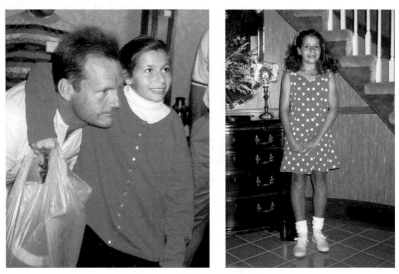

With the Royals' George Brett, left, and dressed in polka-dots.

At Blue Valley North High School, Ali Kemp
played mid-field on the 2000 soccer team.

With Phil Howes, left, and Roger
Kemp, right, Ali held roses as
she was named to the Sweetheart
Court at Blue Valley North.

In high school.

Ali, third from right, with Blue Valley North friends.

Ali and her Dad on moving-in day at Kansas State.

At a Kansas City Royals game, Ali sat with boyfriend Phil Howes

Hours after the murder on June 18, 2002, police began their investigation at Foxborough Pool in Lenexa, Kansas.

In July 2002, John Walsh introduced a nationwide audience to the scene of the crime on "America's Most Wanted."

Benjamin Appleby as a teen, left, and as he appeared on "Wanted" billboards in the Kansas City area.

The house on Bantam Road in Connecticut where
Benjamin Appleby was arrested in November 2004.

Above: Appleby descended
from the airliner that
returned him to Kansas
City. Right: The videotaped
confession shown at his trial.

The Leawood
detective team
(From right):
Major Craig
Hill, Sergeant
Scott Hansen,
John Dickey,
Joe Langer and
Ron Hulsey.

Roger Kemp,
telling a
preliminary
hearing in
September 2005
how he found
Ali's clothing
bunched up
on her body
at the pool.

A dressed-
up Appleby
conferred with
his lawyer.

Left: Instructor Jill Leiker with her husband, Bob Leiker, at an Ali Kemp Foundation self-defense course. Right: Leawood Mayor Peggy Dunn.

Roger Kemp at Ali's graveside in early 2003. Below left: On an anniversary of Ali's death. Below right: Memorial, Tomahawk Creek Park, Leawood, Kansas.

color jokes. Nevertheless, Barr and Appleby saw the Eldringhoffs often. Their small circle of friends gathered on weekends for dinners and parties.

On weekdays, Appleby put in long hours with his Hoover Pool Service taking care of swimming pools for high-income customers, most of them in Johnson County. Evidently, business was good. He often enjoyed a few beers after work, but his favorite drink was Dewar's Scotch on the rocks.

To outward appearances, Appleby had no moral, emotional or ethical regrets about anything in his past. Life went on as normal, and he and Barr continued with their plans to spend the rest of their lives together. Sometime that summer or fall, the couple finalized a date for their wedding. It would take place October 11, 2003, at the White Memorial, a private preserve in Litchfield, Connecticut. Coincidentally, October 11 was Ali Kemp's birthday.

WITHIN A WEEK AFTER ALI KEMP'S DEATH, Leawood police printed posters bearing the illustration of the suspect's face and pickup truck. Working with an army of volunteers, Roger Kemp posted them in stores and malls throughout Leawood and other suburbs. It was important to get the posters out in public as soon as possible.

"The thing he wanted more than anything else," Hill recalled, "was to capture this monster."

Early in July, detectives Hansen and Langer discussed reward money with Kemp. He wanted to put up a large amount right away.

"We said, Let's just try $5,000 and see what we get," Langer recalls. "We didn't want him throwing money out there that we didn't think was necessary and he agreed."

Eventually, the Kemp family increased the reward to $24,000 and the City of Leawood provided, for the first time in its history, an additional $25,000. The idea came from Mayor Peggy Dunn and was approved unanimously by the City Council. The Kansas City Crime Commission added $1,000, bringing the total to $50,000.

Because of the high profile of the Ali Kemp investigation, reporters looking for new developments often called Roger Kemp at his home. Before speaking with the press, Kemp would call Craig Hill of the Leawood police.

"He did not want to say anything," Hill said, "that would at all impair the investigation or upset or anger our investigators." Often, Kemp asked, "what can I say at this point, what should I not say, and is there anything you specifically want me to say to reporters?"

Hill had seen investigations in which a victim's family perceived a lack of progress in a case, grew angry and started publicly blaming the police.

"In Roger's case, he stayed focused on the investigation and was always ready to do what he could to help us," Hill recalled, which was notable because the Kemps' pain was almost beyond enduring.

"This is different from a situation where a victim's parents are notified of the death of a child, but may never see the child," Hill said. Roger Kemp "held in his hands what an assailant had savagely done to his own daughter."

"I could see the pain in his eyes every time I talked with him. I personally couldn't have handled such pain, I am just not tough enough, but Roger did. He is apparently tougher than I am."

When parents become the parents of a murdered child, grief makes its way to the center of their souls; all of life changes. Roger's and Kathy's life went from a world of color to stark black and white. The grass was no longer green, ice cream was no longer flavorful and much of the simple joy of life was gone. The feeling existed day in and day out. The Kemps still had two boys, and they, too, had suffered enormous loss.

"We are just utterly brokenhearted," Kemp said in a media interview shortly after Ali's death. "My wife almost believes that Ali is going to walk through the door or call any second."

In darker moments, they might have asked themselves whether life was worth living. For their sons' sake it certainly was.

"A lot of parents go berserk," Hill said, "commit suicide, start drinking, get a divorce or whatever action they could take to bail themselves out of this horrific feeling. It was entirely different with Roger and Kathy Kemp.

"When Roger got an opportunity to speak, which was often, he did not sensationalize what had happened. He went on day after day, in the very determined hope of seeing that justice would be served. There was never any doubt in my mind that the Kemps would never rest until the suspect was caught, no matter how long it took."

Yet they wanted to go beyond that, Hill recalls, to do something "to be certain that their daughter's name lived on."

IT WAS CLEAR to investigators at the scene of Ali Kemp's death that there had been a terrible struggle. The pump room where the assault took place was torn apart.

"Ali fought and fought for her life," Roger said. "If she had some skills, some training, it might have given her a chance. Ali, like most women, had not been trained in self-defense."

Soon after Ali's death, the Kemps decided to do something to keep a similar tragedy from happening to another girl and another family. They established The Ali Kemp Education Foundation – its acronym was TAKE — as a living memorial to their daughter's life. Its primary purpose was to provide free self-defense classes for women and girls — not only in the Kansas City area but also throughout the United States.

"When we saw the way her death affected us, we knew we had to go out and help other women so it wouldn't happen to them," said Phil Howes, Ali's boyfriend. "It changed all of our lives."

Right away, $10,000 came from Ali's college sorority at Kansas State University, Pi Beta Phi.

"She made a big difference," said sorority member Marti Pries, "so it made it real easy to get the word out and have the money come in."

A group of players from the Kansas City Royals initiated "Rally for Ali" promotion fundraisers. The team's director of community relations, Shani Tate, said, "It was important to us that her family knew that they were not alone in their pain."

A month after her death, high school friends put together a "Light Up the Night for Ali" promotion. Two bands performed with songs that members had written about her, followed by an Alfred

Alfred Angelo fashion show in her honor. Alpha Phi Alpha and LionsGate golf club held golf tournaments for the foundation. Applebee's restaurants raised $2,250 for the foundation by setting up and planning the Ali Kemp Memorial Saturday Night Party; the Blue Valley Car Club sponsored a major car show in the Leawood-Blue Valley area to benefit the fund; Greek organizations at the University of Kansas joined forces to provide funds; a benefit concert in her name was held at Kansas State.

WHEN DETECTIVES RECEIVED LEADS they thought might provide new information to help find the killer, Detective Hansen met with Roger Kemp, telling him about the information yet cautioning him that it might not work out.

Often, it did not.

"Even though he tried not to look disappointed, I am sure it was terribly disappointing to him," Hansen says.

As the investigation went on and on, "there might well have been a time that Roger would have become unhappy with us," Hansen recalled, "and we discussed ways to cope if this happened.

"You know, to Roger's credit, he never did. He stuck with us the whole time."

For his part, Roger Kemp calls Hansen an extreme professional, with emphasis on "extreme."

"Sergeant Hansen was always five steps ahead of everyone else."

He was also even-tempered. Hansen, Kemp says, "kept an eye on everybody and did not let detectives or me get carried away.

"Sometimes I would call him because I had calls at my house, because my name was in the phone book," Kemp recalls, "and a person might say, 'Look I have solved this thing, I called the TIPS Hotline, I called the Leawood Police. I have the name of the man you are looking for.'"

Kemp would relay the message to Hansen. Leawood Police would look into it. Then, Hansen, as the lead detective, would call Roger back. Time and again, he had to say, "Roger, this is what happened, we have checked this person out and it is not he, but we wish it was."

"When Detective Sergeant Hansen would call, and say we think we have a person we should consider," Kemp says, "I would become almost physically sick with anxiety and worry."

If the new information did not lead to the killer or at least shed some light on the search, a new emotional low would hit like a sledgehammer.

"It would last for days and maybe for weeks."

Roger Kemp found that adjusting to the highs and lows was nearly impossible, yet "I knew that I could not afford to let my emotions tear me up like that every time there was bad news."

AFTER POLICE HAD PROCESSED about 900 leads, Langer and Hill went in late August 2002 to El Paso, Texas, to meet with criminal behavior experts at the Federal Bureau of Investigation.

"In spite of all the effort, after all of the work by everyone, we were still not at all sure who or what we were looking for," Hansen says.

FBI staff pored over details of the crime, the victim, the crime scene, the investigation, the evidence gathered to date, the police response that day, the autopsy and DNA findings. Roger Kemp participated in the discussion by speakerphone.

The assailant, the FBI specialists said, might have radically changed his appearance from the police composite poster and he might demonstrate an unusual amount of interest in the investigation. He might be a regular, heavy drinker or he might have started drinking heavily, he might have been a regular smoker or he might have started smoking immediately after the homicide. He might be involved with drugs, might have missed work the week of the homicide, might have some unexplained injuries and probably had changed vehicles.

Also, they said, he might show an unusual amount of hostility toward or lack of respect for women.

By late fall, the assailant seemed to have dropped off the face of the Earth. The small Leawood team, in spite of mistakes and miscues, in spite of one disappointment after another combined with everyday distractions and an unending flow of dead ends, maintained an astonishing focus. The search went on without letup.

"No matter how totally boring or generic or uneventful a lead might appear to be," Hill said, "if there seemed to be just a shred of value — any shred at all — they would spend hours dealing with each. They would stay on each lead and eliminate each one the hard way, one lead at a time.

"I looked at the team that did this investigation every day," Hill said, and "I thought, my God, what if they had taken the easy way out?"

The search led Leawood investigators to Kansas City, to Missouri and Kansas, throughout the Midwest and across the United States. Detectives from Leawood interviewed inmates at city jails, at state and local prisons and at federal penitentiaries. The FBI, the Kansas Bureau of Investigation and police departments nationwide helped in the search. DNA data were transmitted to the Leawood Police Department and then on to the Kansas City, Missouri, Regional Crime Lab or the Johnson Country Crime Lab, where the Ali Kemp investigation was on permanent high-priority status.

THE KEMP FAMILY NEVER STOPPED looking for ways to help.

"We had to have a steady influx of leads," says Roger Kemp. "We wanted leads every day, we had to have them to move forward. Almost any idea under the sun, no matter how remote or off the wall, was on the table at one time or another."

The words he most dreaded were "cold case."

He looked at advertising in magazines with national circulation; after an exhaustive search, none really seemed on target. How much, he wondered, would it cost to put the composite sketch and "wanted" message on the fender or door of a NASCAR racecar, which would reach millions of television viewers as well as thousands of fans in the grandstands every week? Would it be possible to put the message at check-out lanes of major national retail chains?

He thought about placing the suspected killer's face and "wanted" message on film with an audio announcer in movie theatres, as a preview that would run immediately before the feature attraction, to captive theatre audiences across the country.

After a frustrating search through all those possibilities, Roger Kemp found no organization that would do it.

He considered making vinyl signs for display on the back of over-the-road trucks. With this, he had some help. A group of truckers in Kansas City, on their own initiative, put copies of the composite sketches of the suspected killer in truck stops along their routes and made extra copies available for other truckers.

Then one day, as Roger Kemp drove along a familiar expressway leading into south Johnson County, he focused on a couple of billboards.

"The idea hit me," he remembered. "Why not try billboards to display the composite sketch and the 'wanted' message, since so many people drive by billboards every day?"

Hill thought Kemp's idea was perfect:

"It would be awesome. A newspaper, you read it and it's tossed in the trash. Television, it's aired and it's gone. Billboards stand there 24 hours, seven days a week. Nobody had ever used billboards in a criminal investigation before, but it was really worth a try."

That day Kemp called Lamar Outdoor Advertising in Kansas City and asked Account Executive Lea Ann Petrie how much one would cost. Upon learning the caller was Roger Kemp, she replied, "Give us 15 minutes and we will call you back'."

The answer: Lamar would provide the billboards, and would do it for free.

"We had never been approached with an idea like this," said Bob Fessler, Lamar's vice president and general manager in Kansas City. "Some of our boards are dormant at certain times, so why not, we thought, put them to a good use for a cause like this one?

"I thought of my own teenage daughter and the whole idea really hit home with me."

Nevertheless, Fessler was somewhat skeptical:

"We are just putting a sketch up there. It was a good sketch, but it was still a sketch."

The final design included the larger-than-life illustration of the suspect's face and pickup truck, the billboard headline, the Crime Stoppers' TIPS Hotline number and the $50,000 reward.

Roger Kemp had hoped Lamar would provide one billboard. The company provided four, each placed on main expressways across the Kansas City area. The locations rotated every three months. The normal cost for such a billboard would have been $12,000 a month plus about $4,500 for design.

The project represented the first sustained use of billboard advertising in a criminal investigation in the United States.

It was estimated that the campaign produced roughly a quarter-million viewer impressions every day. Response, beginning with the first posting in February of 2003, was immediate and sustained.

"We knew," recalls Roger Kemp, "that we were on to something."

So successful was the publicity campaign, in fact, that detectives worried about the large volume of leads.

"All of us were working on the case full-time," said Leawood Detective Joe Langer. "We did not want to get a lead, any lead, and not give it complete follow-up. We didn't want to get the main lead — wherever it was, whenever it was, the big blockbuster lead that would lead us to the killer — and then miss it because we were too busy. Sometimes it was a Catch–22. At any one time, we probably had enough leads and tips for 25 detectives."

Amid the flood of leads after the billboards went up was one that went to the TIPS Hotline, which faxed it to Leawood police at 1:45 p.m. on February 14, 2003. It did not appear, at first glance, to be of unusual importance.

According to the TIPS operator's narrative, the caller described a white male, about 5 feet, 8 inches tall, in his 30s with a stocky build.

"Caller stated that a Ben Hoover, who owns Hoover Pool Service in KCK, looks like the composite. He also fits the physical description."

This lead, like all the others, was entered in the database. A hard copy was placed chronologically in one of the case's binders for follow-up.

FOLLOWING UP TIPS WAS HARD WORK, most often frustrating and sometimes bizarre.

In 2002, Leawood Detective John Dickey drove to Excelsior Springs, Missouri, about 60 miles northeast of Leawood. At the address, a long dirt driveway led down to a trailer parked in the middle of a field. A truck was parked next to the trailer. The front door of the trailer was open. "I looked up and saw this guy," Dickey recalled. "Then I saw a television set in the back of the truck and it kind of looked like a burglary." Dickey got out of the car and announced that he was working on the Ali Kemp investigation.

"As we talked, I noticed that he put his hands in his pockets. He seemed very frightened and not really there. He came over and sat down in my car and told me that he was the Lamb of God and that he talked to God."

Dickey nodded. Could he get a DNA sample?

That was "a way-out question," Dickey said, "and I knew we were not on the same wavelength. I decided to leave. As I was backing out the driveway I saw that person standing there staring at me and then he ran back to the shed and it looked as if he was going to get a weapon. So I just took off and later got his DNA through his parents."

Later, Dickey discovered that the individual was going through a divorce and "at one point he was driving his wife's car, put on a football helmet and drove her car off a bridge and we learned he was never the same after that."

Another tip led detectives to an auto repair shop in Olathe, Kansas, where a suspect's onetime employer told them he was at work the day of Ali Kemp's death.

"This is a 2-person shop, and I am the boss," the employer said. "I would know if he wasn't here."

The trail cooled for a few months, when the same suspect was charged with kidnapping and rape in three separate incidents in Kansas and Missouri. The man had an uncanny resemblance to the composite illustration of the suspect in Ali Kemp's slaying, he had served time for other crimes of violence, and he was wanted for assaults against women. Captured in Utah in early 2003, he was brought back to Kansas City and his DNA taken.

In February 2003 a woman told the TIPS Hotline about a man who had approached her at a suburban branch library. Did she think he looked sexy? he asked, telling her she was at a good age and that he carried bedding with him. He told her he would be back at the same library a few days later. According to the caller, he resembled the composite on the billboard.

Detectives went to his apartment in Leawood and knocked. When the door opened, they found the man wearing no clothes. He allowed them to take a DNA sample. Three weeks later, a hand-addressed envelope arrived at police headquarters. On a slip of paper inside was written, "Do the DNA results disprove the allegations of that insecure, judgmental bitch?"

After months of fruitless inquiries, John Walsh suggested placing ads in USA Today. The paper claimed more than two million paid subscribers nationwide, with a combined readership approaching four million. It seemed like a good option, although an expensive one.

"I thought about it for about two weeks," Roger Kemp recalls. "Then I made the decision that I was not going to someday look back — two years, five years or whatever — and say I wish I had done that; I wish I had turned that stone over."

Half-page ads ran in April 2003. The TIPS Hotline reported only a slight increase in leads, but the ads brought a tantalizing response from an inmate at a Texas prison. In letters to Texas authorities, he said he knew who was responsible for killing Ali Kemp, a man named "Rick." At the time of the murder, the inmate wrote, this man was out of prison and in a Kansas town, probably Leawood.

"He used to park at a swimming pool to watch girls while he took his lunch breaks." the inmate said of "Rick." He added that "Rick was a "sexual pervert" and that the artist's sketch he had seen in USA Today "looks exactly like him; this is him!" On the letter's second page, the inmate wrote, "there was one girl working at the pool that really excited him." This girl had long black hair, and in the inmate's opinion, matched the description of Ali Kemp. Not surprisingly, the inmate then added that he "would like to be considered for the reward money."

Detectives Langer and Hansen flew to Texas the next week and interviewed the inmate in a holding room at the prison. Afterward, authorities tracked down "Rick" and checked his DNA profile.

Multiple airings of the Ali Kemp story on "America's Most Wanted" provided a seemingly endless supply of tips. One tip brought up the name of "David," who was in jail in Colorado Springs, Colorado. According to the tipster, he "looks very much like the sketch of the suspect in Ali Kemp's murder."

The arrest photo of "David" bore a remarkable resemblance to the composite, detectives agreed. Colorado authorities knew "David" to be extremely violent. He was known to have stolen a tan Ford pickup from a construction site some time in the past. He had a sometime girlfriend in St. Joseph, Missouri, about 75 miles from Leawood, and she said "David" had visited her in summer 2002.

The case of a Nebraska man who was a convicted sexual sadist and a suspect in four serial killings of female victims came to the attention of Leawood investigators in summer 2003. He was scheduled for sentencing in a sexual assault on his stepdaughter, women's underwear was found in his bedroom and he owned a tan 1980s Ford pickup.

Detectives Dickey and Langer interviewed the man at the Nebraska State Penitentiary Diagnostic Center. He said he had been in Nebraska on the day Ali Kemp was slain, but acknowledged he had been in the Kansas suburbs of Kansas City earlier in June 2002. He gave a DNA sample.

In the case of the Nebraska convict, as with "David" in Colorado Springs, and "Rick" in Texas, and the suspicious man at the library, and the auto mechanic from Olathe, and the Lamb of

God in Excelsior Springs, and in all the other leads that looked so promising for a while, DNA samples simply did not match the one left by Ali Kemp's assailant.

The man they wanted was still at large.

The Ali Kemp story, with updates, was aired again on "America's Most Wanted" on April 12, 2003. As Joe Langer remembers, "I think we broke the record again for incoming calls and we did equally well with TIPS Hotline. So we got a lot more leads from that second show. The leads were just as well received. The investigation continued for all of us without interruption."

O N MAY 24, 2003, ELEVEN MONTHS after the homicide, the Leawood swimming pool was reopened with new security measures in place. Members would now need electronic cards to enter the pool complex. Employees would carry panic alarms to contact an alarm monitoring company. Geoffrey Login, board president of the Foxborough homeowners association, said two employees would always be a work at any time — never again would a solitary attendant be on duty.

B Y JUNE 18, 2003, LEAWOOD DETECTIVES had been working on the Ali Kemp homicide for a full year; more than 1,000 leads and tips had been examined, one lead at a time. Many were cursory. Most work involved the elimination of suspects.

On the day of the slaying's one-year anniversary, a person called the Leawood investigators directly, telling them that they should concern themselves with one Teddy L. Hoover. He lived at 49 South 64th Street in Kansas City, Kansas, and operated his own swimming pool maintenance company. Hoover's girlfriend, the caller said, was named Lara Barr. Hoover was self-employed with his own swimming pool service company. He once lived in Connecticut and sometimes went by the name "Ben." He had a violent temper. The caller said that Hoover's dad had an old pickup truck and recalled that it was beige. Hoover was known to occasionally drive the vehicle. Hoover, the caller said, looked like the composite.

The lead was placed for follow-up with others.

On September 9, 2003, Sergeant Hansen drove up to the house at 49 South 64th Street in Kansas City, Kansas. In the driveway sat a reddish pickup truck filled with pool chemicals.

At home he found the man known as Teddy Hoover. He was cooperative at first. Hansen mentioned that the Hoover name had been called in twice by tipsters, a comment that his interviewee seemed to ignore. He said his name was Ted L. Hoover and his date of birth was July 11, 1974, Hansen reported, adding that "he said he was self-employed and had his own swimming pool maintenance business. He explained that he was up and down State Line Road all the time and he had several customers in the Leawood area."

On June 18, 2002, "he said that he would have been working at one of the pools he services, but he could not verify which one or exactly where he had been that day."

Would he be willing to provide a DNA sample? Not without speaking to his attorney, John Quinn.

Fine, Hansen told him, but the only way he could be eliminated as a suspect would be to provide his DNA. The interviewee's refusal was not unusual; even people under questioning for a crime for which they were innocent feared that a DNA sample would point authorities to a crime that they had actually committed. Without a warrant, Hansen could not force Appleby to provide a sample.

Back at the office, Hansen ran a computer check of the Kansas City metropolitan area on the name Ted Hoover. He found no significant criminal record.

The next month, Hansen spoke with the lawyer, John Quinn. Quinn said his client was worried that a DNA sample would be put in a database. Hansen faxed to Quinn a letter promising that police would use the results only in connection with the Ali Kemp case. On October 8 or 9, 2003, Quinn told his client about the letter and said the two needed to pay Hansen a visit. That was their last communication.

When the Leawood detectives checked back with Quinn, they were told his client had gone to Las Vegas, Nevada, to look for work. Calling his landlord, they were told the man known as

Teddy Hoover might have gone to Florida with his girlfriend.

"I think they are trying to stir up something from my past," Appleby had told a friend, "and I'm a little worried about it."

ON NOVEMBER 4, 2003, A CALLER to Kansas City's TIPS Hotline once again connected the name "Hoover" to the slaying of Ali Kemp. The message was abrupt. According to the operator's transcript, it said, "Suspect is a contractor who works on pools and drives a beat up old red truck and a beige truck. He has the following telephone numbers: Cell 913-207-4569, home 913-287-7191. Suspect originally from CT. The week after the homicide, suspect had a homemade cast on one of his hands. Suspect looks just like the composite on the billboards. Suspect is heavy set."

Like the first tip, which arrived in February 2003, the first name of Hoover was given as "Ben." The second tip, which came in June, called him "Ted." In the passage of time and the confusion of first names, the tips remained only part of a sea of possibilities for police.

Sergeant Craig Sarver, coordinator of the Greater Kansas City Crime Stoppers, managed the TIPS Hotline leads generated by the billboards.

"We had no idea over here of the total significance of those particular leads," he says. "At the time, we were still sending four or five tips each day to Leawood. They still had to sort out, analyze and follow up on all of those ongoing leads as well as these new ones."

BY NOVEMBER 2003, BENJAMIN APPLEBY AND LARA BARR were back in Connecticut. Their first address was 19 New Milford Turnpike in New Preston Marble Dale, the home of Lara Barr's mother and stepfather. Appleby went to work as an installer for his stepfather's Jalbert Roofing and Framing.

That arrangement would last about eight months. Then, Appleby and Barr moved to a small blue cottage at 1210 Bantam Road in Bantam, Connecticut, a quiet borough of modest homes in Litchfield County, about 8 miles from New Preston Marble Dale.

Barr found a job with an area veterinary office. Appleby opened a new swimming pool maintenance business, printed business cards and put the company name, Preferred Pools, on his pick-up truck. He made no secret of the fact that he was from Kansas City.

THE INVESTIGATION CONTINUED INTO 2004, and leads and tips were still arriving at Leawood Police headquarters every day from across the country. The database, with leads now numbering in the thousands, was in constant use. Meetings at headquarters still monitored progress every morning. New leads were assigned to detectives. Follow-up was constant on days, nights and weekends.

In June, investigators traveled again to Kansas State University in Manhattan. They hoped to gather information from Ali's sorority sisters and other people she had known on campus that might have seemed unimportant in 2002. A few new leads were inconsequential. That same month, the Leawood City Council voted unanimously to support Mayor Peggy Dunn's recommendation to continue the agreement with the Kansas City Metropolitan Crime Commission until the end of June 2005 to make available $25,000 to the Greater Kansas City Crime Stoppers TIPS Hotline. The council vote was unanimous.

By fall 2004, the marathon investigation appeared to have no end in sight. Six Leawood detectives working fulltime had investigated more than 1,300 leads. Forty new leads arrived each week; much of the work still involved elimination of suspects. The quality of leads still varied considerably.

Detectives had been to Las Vegas, Houston, South Carolina, Colorado Springs, Washington, D.C., Chicago, Wichita, Springfield, Topeka, Omaha, Leavenworth and other points throughout the Midwest. They met in Washington with investigators who had worked on serial homicide cases involving Ted Bundy and the Green River killer. By early October, DNA profiles had been established for about 900 men; some demanded a consent form confirming that their DNA would only be used in this investigation; others refused to provide DNA samples at all.

The files of some, but not all who had refused to provide DNA were moved up in priority. One of those was the file of the man they knew only as Teddy Hoover.

8

Closing In

*"That certainly raised his importance. Before, he was an important
lead among hundreds."*
— Detective Sergeant Scott Hansen, on hearing
of suspect's sex crimes

In October 2004, Detective Joe Langer was reviewing files, still
narrowing the field of suspects, when he decided to check on the
whereabouts of Teddy Hoover. Hoover had been interviewed a
year before, but had left town for parts unknown. However he was
known to have lived with a woman named Lara Barr in Kansas City,
Kansas. Where was she now?

Langer contacted authorities at the U.S. Postal Service. They
reported a Lara Barr at 1210 Bantam Road in Bantam, Connecticut.
A man was also receiving mail at that address, they said, but his
name was not Teddy Hoover. It was Benjamin Appleby.

Was he the same man? Was it time to pay him a visit?

On October 20, 2004, Detective Hansen called Daniel Jewiss,
an investigator with the Western District Major Crime Squad of the
Connecticut State Police in Litchfield, Connecticut.

"We have a homicide case," Hansen told him. "One of the guys
we interviewed took off on us. We feel he has moved up into your
area. Can you run by the house where we think he might be staying
and see if you can establish whether or not this guy is there before
we come up there?"

Absolutely, Jewiss said, and asked Hansen for a case summary.
Hansen sent it the same day. In it, Teddy L. Hoover was listed as
a "prime" suspect in the slaying of Ali Kemp. Police were growing
more interested, but Hoover remained one of many in whom they

were interested.

Two days later, Jewiss drove by 1210 Bantam Road and saw two vehicles in the gravel driveway: a gray, two-door Buick Sedan registered to Lara Barr and a black 2002 Kia Sportage sport utility vehicle registered to Ina E. Barr-Jalbert, Barr's mother. Although Jewiss did not see a man there, his department checked its database for the name Teddy Hoover.

On October 24, Jewiss sent Hansen a 24-page fax. It contained stunning news.

The Teddy Hoover about whom Leawood was inquiring was the object of a five-year-old arrest warrant accusing him of exposing himself in 1997 in Woodbury and New Milford, Connecticut. Also, the fax detailed how Hoover had confessed to a similar crime in 1998 in New Milford.

For the first time, Leawood police knew that the person calling himself Teddy Hoover had a history of sexual misconduct.

"That certainly raised his importance," Hansen recalls. "Before, he was an important lead among hundreds."

Now the name Hoover rose closer to the top of their list. In the three telephone tips received in 2003 about someone named Hoover, the first name had been given twice as "Ben" and only once as "Teddy." Policeman Lasley — who in the hours after Ali's death had listed someone named Teddy Hoover as one of the people who left the Foxborough pool parking lot — had written his cell phone number as 913-488-1190. Yet one of the tipsters who named "Ben" Hoover gave a different cell phone number.

The Leawood detectives needed some bit of information that would give them a better fix on the suspect. In the first week of November, that something arrived. In their daily meeting, detectives continued to ask themselves: What have we not done? Why haven't we found him?

That day Detective Ron Hulsey, still willing to try anything, said he was going to pore through traffic accident reports. Why? "Just on the chance," Hulsey said, "that maybe the bad guy was in an accident."

He came upon one that sounded interesting. It had occurred December 17, 2001, at 8700 State Line Road. That afternoon, a drunken driver's vehicle had collided with a maroon Ford pickup truck. The driver of the pickup gave his name to Leawood policewoman Dianna Johnson as Teddy L. Hoover II. He told her his business phone number was 913-488-1190. Hulsey read the number to Hansen. It caught their attention. They compared it with the cellphone number given to officer Lasley at the crime scene parking lot on June 18, 2002, the day of Ali Kemp's slaying. The numbers matched.

For the first time, they had the name Ted – or Teddy – Hoover on two separate occasions alongside the same phone number. Quickly, the man who called himself Teddy Hoover became No. 1 on their list.

To Hansen, it was time to act. He gave Major Hill a rundown: Based on what they had learned from Connecticut, Teddy Hoover had a sex-crime history. Hoover might be the same man as Benjamin Appleby, a man postal authorities had found was receiving mail at 1210 Bantam Road in Bantam, Connecticut. That was the residence of Lara Barr, known to be Teddy Hoover's longtime girlfriend. The Crime Stoppers tip of February 14, 2003, described a "Ben Hoover, who owns Hoover Pool Service in KCK, looks like the composite and fits the physical description." The phone tip called into police headquarters on June 18, 2003, had said Hoover looked like the composite, had a "violent temper," also, "goes by Ben, used to live in Connecticut," and occasionally drove what the caller recalled as a beige pickup truck. The man called Teddy Hoover whom Hansen interviewed in Kansas City, Kansas, on September 9, 2003, had said he was often in Leawood servicing pool customers in summer 2002. He could not explain where he was on the day of the homicide. He had refused to provide a DNA and had left the area. The Crime Stopper's tip of November 4, 2003, said Hoover "drives a beat-up old red truck and occasionally drives a beige truck," and "looks like the composite on the billboard." According to that caller, a week after the homicide the "suspect had a homemade cast on one hand."

Hansen wanted to take three detectives to Connecticut.

"If Hoover did not cooperate and if we cannot get a search warrant for his DNA," Hansen recalled, "we were going to have to try to follow this guy until we could get his DNA. Then if it didn't match we would come home, but if it did match we didn't want him sitting around waiting for the match to come back."

Major Craig Hill's decision was immediate. He told Hansen to go with the other three detectives to Connecticut, and to do so as fast as possible. Hill made one phone call, sent an e-mail and appropriated the funds. The four Leawood detectives would leave for Connecticut on Sunday, November 7.

John Dickey had just returned from a police class in Las Vegas. Hansen called him and said, "Hey John, we are going to Connecticut." Dickey replied, "I said, OK, have a good time."

Hansen replied: "No, you are going with us. Things are starting to look a little better with Teddy Hoover; things are looking better all the time."

Hansen and detectives Langer, Dickey and Hulsey would make the trip.

In anticipation of a face-to-face interview with Hoover, Langer spoke with a member of the police homicide unit in Kansas City, Missouri, who recommended using props. Following that advice, Leawood police created charts linking Hoover to the crime scene, an enlarged copy of Hoover's driver's license, a picture of Ali Kemp, an aerial view of the Foxborough swimming pool complex, a VCR tape labeled "Foxborough Pool," a copy of Ali Kemp's obituary mounted on white poster board paper, and autopsy photos. Other props included a large poster with the suspect's picture in the center surrounded by facts about the case that made him a prime suspect, a timeline marking the date of the homicide, the progress of the investigation and the suspect's known movements. Also, they prepared a black notebook labeled "HOOVER, TEDDY L., AKA APPLEBY, BENJAMIN, W/M: 7/11/74," and a second notebook labeled "Crime Scene Photos."

Everything was designed to show the suspect how police connected him to the Ali Kemp homicide.

"We had really orchestrated the whole situation," Dickey said. "Before we went, we had time to sit down and game-plan. Part of that was for Joe Langer and me to talk to the suspect and build a rapport with him."

In Connecticut, meanwhile, state police were keeping an eye on 1210 Bantam Road. About 12:45 p.m. on November 5, detectives drove past the residence — a small, one-story, single-family dwelling painted blue with white trim. No vehicles were parked in its gravel driveway. At 6 p.m. that day, a detective drove by the residence again and reported seeing a heavyset woman with shoulder-length hair on the deck outside the house. The next morning, another drive past the residence found a red 1996 Ford F-150 pickup and a gray Buick Riviera in the gravel driveway. Both vehicles were registered to Lara Barr.

By this time Connecticut police, using their computer database, had linked the name Teddy Hoover to Benjamin Appleby. They also found that Appleby had been associated with Barr since early 1998.

THE FOUR LEAWOOD DETECTIVES ARRIVED in Connecticut on Sunday night. The next morning, November 8, 2004, they went to the State Police Barracks in Litchfield. From there, Connecticut police drove them in an unmarked squad car past the house at 1210 Bantam Road, only about three miles from the State Police offices. A pickup truck was in the driveway, but it did not appear anyone was at home. A surveillance vehicle was set up near the house.

Later that morning, Leawood Detective Langer and Connecticut Detective Jewiss drafted a warrant to search the house and to obtain a DNA profile from the man who lived there. At 2:20 that afternoon, at the courthouse in Litchfield, Superior Court Judge Robert A. Brunetti issued a warrant. It authorized detectives to enter the dwelling at 1210 Bantam Road in Bantam, Connecticut, and provided broad authority for detectives to search the residence and seize items that "may constitute evidence related to the commission of Felony Murder." It also authorized swabbings for DNA from "Teddy L. Hoover II, (AKA Benjamin Appleby) a Caucasian male with the birth date of July 11, 1974."

The plan was for Connecticut officials to arrest Appleby on the 1997 warrant charging him with public indecency in the incidents at Nonnewaug and New Milford high schools. They would take him to the State Police barracks, charge him with those crimes, and then deliver him to an interrogation room to meet with the Leawood detectives.

Events moved swiftly.

At 2:36 p.m. officers in the surveillance vehicle watching the residence on Bantam Road reported that a man had pulled into the driveway and entered the house. At 2:50 p.m. Sergeant David DelVecchia, criminal investigations supervisor with the State Police, left the Troop L barracks. DelVecchia had the 1997 warrant and the two search warrants in hand. Six state police accompanied him.

At 1210 Bantam Road, they surrounded the house. DelVecchia, wearing a State Police raid jacket, went to the side door, which was close to the driveway, and knocked.

A man came to the door.

"He let me in," DelVecchia recalls. "He looked like he was working on something. He had a screwdriver in his hand. I identified myself."

DelVecchia asked him to put down the screwdriver and told him he had an arrest warrant for Teddy Hoover. The man said his name was Appleby, not Hoover, and did not know who Hoover was. He retrieved an identification card with the name Benjamin Appleby.

From photographs, DelVecchia knew that Appleby and Hoover were the same person. He did not did know whether the man's name was really Appleby or Hoover, but he knew that he was the subject of the warrant. He arrested him, handcuffed him and led him to his squad car.

Leawood police detectives remained in a separate squad car on a side street, a block away. They watched as police escorted him out of the house and frisked him.

"We didn't want Appleby to know that Leawood, Kansas, was even there," Hansen said. "The longer he thought this was a Connecticut matter only, the better."

Detective Jewiss, followed by a uniformed officer in another squad car, drove the suspect to the police barracks. During the ride Appleby told Jewiss that his name really was Benjamin Appleby, but that he had often used the name Teddy Hoover, his dead childhood friend. He asked why his house was being searched. Jewiss told him that police were doing it under a search warrant unrelated to his arrest.

"I also explained to him that he would definitely be told more about his arrest and the search warrant at a later time," Jewiss recalls, "but right then I could not talk to him about it."

At 3:38 p.m. they arrived at the State Police barracks. Appleby was taken out of the police car and his handcuffs were removed. He was photographed. Finger and palm prints were taken. He measured 5 feet 9 inches tall and weighed about 250 pounds. He had a scar on his right shoulder, a sun tattoo on his chest and a tribal design tattoo on his right arm. His personal property was listed.

Jewiss read to him the Connecticut Superior Court's Notice of Rights, which included the right to remain silent, the right to consult with an attorney before being questioned, the right to say nothing regarding the offense with which he was being charged, and the right not to be questioned without his consent. Jewiss asked Appleby whether he understood. Appleby said that he did and signed the Notice of Rights form. Appleby asked whether he would be able to speak to a lawyer at some point and Jewiss said that he would.

About 3:55 p.m. Detective Raymond Insalaco of the State Police was asked to go to the prisoner processing room to take swabs from Appleby. Insalaco had done this hundreds of times with other people. The procedure was simple. Wearing rubber gloves, Insalaco opened a sterile package holding the swabs, which resembled Q-Tips inside a container. He pushed on a rod, knocking off a plastic cap and the swab emerged untouched by Insalaco.

"What is this for?" Appleby asked. "What is going on? What are you doing?"

The suspect, Insalaco recalls, "turned red, blue and pale. You could tell he was scared."

Insalaco and Jewis had seen prisoners terrified of DNA many times before.

"Can I say no?" Appleby asked. "Should I have an attorney for this?"

Insalaco replied, "I have a valid search warrant signed by Superior Court Judge Robert A. Brunetti on this date, November 8, 2004, and I'll be taking swabs." There was no question about it.

"If I say no," Appleby asked, "is this go time?"

"Whatever you want it to be," Insalaco said. The men stared at each other for about 30 seconds and then Appleby said "Go ahead, take them."

Six swabs were taken, touched only by the inside of Appleby's mouth. Each was placed in an individual container. Each container was sealed with red evidence tape. Each was initialed "RI" by Insalaco on evidence stickers on each side of a white container. They were placed inside individual envelopes. The time was 3:59 p.m.

The completed and packaged swabbings, identified as State's Exhibits 11-A and 11-B, were given to Leawood Detective Hansen. He identified the package with his initials, "SH" and badge number 169, placed two of the six swabs in a FedEx tube and addressed the package to the Leawood Police Department, to the attention of Major Hill.

They had to move fast. Detectives were not sure how long Connecticut officials could hold Appleby on the misdemeanor charge. The Johnson County Crime Lab had told the detectives that if DNA package arrived the next morning, November 9, Appleby's results could be rushed thorough the same day.

"We missed the FedEx guy at the store," Hansen explains, "because it was after 5 by the time we got there. We saw a FedEx truck on the street. Sergeant DelVecchia turned on the siren and lights and the FedEx driver almost went off the road. She stopped at the curb and we gave her the DNA package and it was on its way."

Meanwhile, Leawood Detective Ron Hulsey searched the house on Bantam Road. Among other things, he found IRS paperwork belonging to Benjamin Appleby, a wrench with the name "Hoover" etched on it, a Kansas drivers license issued to Teddy L. Hoover II, a Preferred Pools fax cover sheet, and an envelope containing personal identification paperwork and birth certificates for

Benjamin Allen Appleby. Hulsey also found an old red letterman's jacket. "Ben" was embroidered on the front and it bore a tag with the name Ben Appleby.

At 4:09 p.m. Detective Jewiss told Appleby that a couple of other detectives wanted to talk to him about things unrelated to his arrest. Fine, Appleby said. Jewiss escorted Appleby up the stairs to an interview room on the second floor at the Connecticut State Police office.

There, Leawood detectives John Dickey and Joe Langer introduced themselves. Dickey advised Appleby of his Miranda rights and asked whether he understood. Appleby said that he did.

Would he agree to waive those rights and speak with them? The subject, Langer told him, would be the Ali Kemp homicide. Someone had called in his name as a suspect, Langer continued, and they were sure that he wanted to clear the matter up.

Appleby said he would talk with them — in fact, wanted to speak with them. Langer and Dickey had planned for an hourlong, non-confrontational interview.

They wanted Appleby to talk about himself, "to see what he would tell us," Langer said. If it was obvious Appleby was lying, "we wouldn't confront him with that fact during the first interview. There were no threats or promises of any kind."

"These types of persons love to talk about themselves," Dickey said. "They love it if you show any interest in them at all, which we did. Did you grow up in Kansas City? What school did you go to? Who did you hang out with? They will go on and on."

Even as the first interview was ending, Langer said, "We would continue to listen to his obvious lies" and then in the second interview detectives would confront him with those lies "so that he would be on the record as lying to us."

Almost certainly, Appleby knew that he was in serious trouble.

"You guys are not going to release me until my DNA comes back?" he asked. That's correct, the detectives said. Langer and Dickey asked him whether he needed to go to the restroom or wanted a drink of water. No, Appleby said, he was fine.

Then he was moved to a room down the hall, where the interview would become more direct. There, detectives had placed the props brought with them from Leawood — among them the chart linking him to the Ali Kemp homicide. Appleby was stunned by what he saw.

Detectives wasted little time.

Langer asked Appleby to tell them where he was on the day of Ali Kemp's murder, June 18, 2002.

"He thought for a minute and then told us he believed on the day of the homicide that he was working at a Hallbrook residence." He named its owners.

"Are you sure about that?" Langer asked. Appleby nodded.

Dickey raised questions about the possibility that Appleby's DNA had been found at the crime scene. Appleby said he had never been to the Foxborough pool that day or any other, so any DNA could not be his. He said he was not worried about that. He was sure a DNA test would clear him.

At one point, he said that he might have serviced a pool near 123rd and State Line Road, but he thought it was a pool at 127th Street and State Line.

What about the name Ted Hoover, which was on the list of those leaving the pool parking lot on June 18, 2002? Langer reminded him how he had given his name and phone number to Leawood policeman Rodman Lasley, who canvassed the names of people in the parking lot that night.

Appleby was shocked. Dickey looked directly at him — and told him he had lied about never being at the pool.

"Oh, I forgot that," Appleby replied. "I just remembered, now that you told me about this incident, that I was there and that I was at a family's house in Leawood talking to them, trying to get them as clients to do work on their pool."

Appleby said that he had driven past 123rd Street and State Line Road, seen the commotion and decided to stop. He apologized for not remembering his visit before being confronted about it.

The detectives looked at him and shook their heads. Things were adding up, they told Appleby, and it didn't look good for him. They said they didn't believe most of what he was saying.

The fact that he left town after Hansen interviewed him in September 2003, the fact that he lied about being at the pool on June 18 and the fact that he changed his name — all of it seemed questionable. Appleby said he knew it didn't look good, but that he had finished work that day and gone home, cleaned up, changed his clothes, changed cars and then driven Lara Barr's gray Buick Riviera back to Leawood to interview a potential customer. It was then, he said, that he saw the hubbub at the pool and decided to stop.

It seemed strange, detectives said, to drive all the way from Leawood to Kansas City, Kansas, to "change clothes to talk to a client" and then return to Leawood.

Dickey cut to the finish.

"We've got your DNA," he told Appleby, "and it's going to come back."

He paused, and then asked Appleby directly: Did you kill Ali Kemp?

Appleby looked away and down and said that he had not. Dickey pressed him on the details of the chart linking him to the crime and on his previous lies.

Abruptly, Appleby shouted, "I killed her!"

The room fell silent, the detectives recall, for long minutes. Appleby began to cry and said he didn't deserve to live; he wanted to kill himself "but he didn't have a gun and he didn't have the guts."

The detectives weren't fooled: "He tried to manipulate us into feeling sorry for him."

Appleby told them he wanted to plead guilty. Langer said they wanted specific information about the homicide.

"'What difference did it make?'" Langer recalls his saying. "'I killed her.'" Dickey replied that exact information about the crime might "help the Kemp family deal with why he killed their daughter."

Appleby relented, and told his story.

On the afternoon of the murder, he said, he was driving down State Line Road and saw the Foxborough pool at 123rd Street. He decided to try to contact someone at the pool in hopes of making a bid for the maintenance contract. As he drove into the parking lot he noticed two men doing yard work nearby.

Picking up his five-gallon carryall containing chemicals and an assortment of tools, he walked through the gate and to the pool. He stopped, looked at the pool and then turned and saw Ali Kemp in the pump room. He walked over and stood in the doorway. He thought she was very attractive. He decided on the spot that he would ask her for a date. He hoped to have sex with her. He began to talk, but she was not interested.

Detectives listened as he continued with his story. It was about 6:30 p.m. when Appleby finished.

The interview room fell silent. Langer and Dickey looked at each other. After 29 months of soul-searching, after one disappointment after another, they had the predator who had eluded them for so long.

Langer asked Appleby what he had used to strangle the victim. Appleby said he did not remember.

Would Appleby make a videotaped statement? He agreed.

About 30 minutes later, in yet another interview room, with a video recorder running, Appleby made the confession that would be entered as State Exhibit 17 at his trial.

Investigators had rarely seen anything like it. Appleby appeared on camera in a black T-shirt. He did not look into the camera. He rubbed his hands and arms cross the table. He broke down and cried and covered his face with his hands.

"I went in there to the pool to get the business," he sobbed. "I'd never seen her before. I did not go in there with the intention of doing what I did."

His approach to Ali Kemp in the pump room, he realized, had made her apprehensive. She wanted nothing to do with him. When she tried to leave, he reached for her. She punched him. He lost his temper.

"I hit her back," he said. "I hit her a few times and we fell down to the floor." During the struggle, his five-gallon carryall was knocked over; his tools were scattered across the pump room floor.

He wiped his eyes. He said he strangled her, but could not

remember what he used. He tore off some of her clothing, but was unable to have sex with her.

Then he had a "moment of clarity." Panicking, he gathered up his tools and some of her clothes and put them in his carryall bucket and left the pump room.

Sobbing, he said: "I thought she was still alive. I heard her breathing; I thought she said something so I stopped. The floor was cold, so I put the f—— cover on her. I thought she was OK so, you know, I just laid it on her. I didn't want anybody to find her like that, I didn't think she was dead."

Detective Dickey said: "OK, Ben, some things I just want to get clear in my mind. Detective Langer and I spoke to you earlier. Did we promise you anything?"

"No," Appleby replied, "you haven't promised me anything or coerced me in any way."

By then, it was about 7:30 p.m. Appleby asked whether he could call his parents. Dickey gave him a phone, but told Appleby he would have to be there while he talked. Appleby tried to call his mother but she was not at home. He reached his father, Gary Appleby, and said: "Dad, they got me. Fill in the blanks." The remark led investigators to believe that Gary Appleby had known from Day One that his son killed Ali Kemp.

Next, Lara Barr was allowed into the interview room. As the detectives watched, Appleby told her what he had done.

"We felt really bad for her," Langer remembers. "Could you imagine that you were in love with someone and you thought you were going to have a life with them and then found out that person had killed somebody in a horrific murder?"

The two Leawood detectives were exhausted. Langer described the feeling as dark and overpowering, "like you have been sitting in the room with the devil incarnate. It was truly a dark, sinister feeling, very hard to describe and we were very tired, but we had him, after all that time. By God, we finally had him."

Appleby was crying, but they knew it was because he had been caught. They guessed that he didn't love Lara Barr. He appeared to have no remorse for Ali Kemp.

Hansen called Major Hill in Leawood. That night Hill and

Police Chief Sid Mitchell went to the Kemp family home.

The feeling, Roger Kemp recalls, was "enormously bittersweet... elation and a terrible sadness all at the same time."

"The fact that this predator did what he did to another human being, to Ali, makes you sick," Kemp said, "and now he has a name."

Appleby was taken to the prisoner holding area where processing was completed. He was placed in a cell. An extraditable warrant for felony murder was issued by the Leawood Police Department. His bond was set at $1 million.

A T LEAWOOD POLICE HEADQUARTERS at 8:30 the morning of November 9, Detective Bill Burke picked up the overnight package from Connecticut, a tube with red evidence tape on both ends. He placed the case number, his initials, a property slip number and the item number on the tube and rushed it to the Johnson County Crime Lab in Mission, Kansas. Since the crime in 2002, the lab had kept at least two DNA samples belonging to a Caucasian male, samples found in the pool's pump room on an antibiotic ointment tube and its cap.

Meanwhile, in Connecticut, the four Leawood detectives headed for Hartford to board a flight home. At their layover in Detroit, Hansen called police headquarters in Leawood.

The Crime Lab's work was done, he was told, and the DNA matched.

"That was just icing on the cake," Hansen recalls. "We had a small party in the Detroit airport."

The news of Appleby's capture spread rapidly. For Leawood, it was electrifying. At police headquarters, recalls department secretary Alison Wacker, "It is hard to explain how emotionally excited we all were. The guys had worked so hard and so long with so many disappointments."

Leawood Mayor Peggy Dunn was at a business conference in Branson, Missouri, when she got word from City Administrator Scott Lambers. Many of the attendees at the conference had teenagers or college students.

"I saw their relief and joy," Dunn said. "All of us were so on edge until he was found. Everyone had felt violated by this crime."

Shortly, word reached Ali's sorority sisters at Kansas State and other friends there and at the University of Kansas, and Lee Hammond, the artist who donated her own time to create the Appleby composite illustration. In Smithville, Missouri, a group of business associates of Roger Kemp went from store to store to announce that Appleby had been caught.

At "America's Most Wanted" headquarters in Washington, staff was euphoric. Appleby's name was quickly posted along with the names of other captured criminals in the conference room. John Walsh was profoundly moved: "What all of us have wanted is justice, just simple justice, and now that will happen."

At the Ali Kemp Foundation, Jill Leiker and her staff had waited months for this.

"We are doing all of our work to honor Ali, to honor her life," she said, "and we know, of course, that nothing can bring her back to us, but now at least there will be some measure of justice for Roger and Kathy and the boys."

The news also went quickly to Craig Sarver and the staff of Crime Stoppers of Kansas City who had taken their largest-ever volume of calls regarding a single crime. Major Hill told Sarver, "Your two tips helped us enormously."

At Lamar Outdoor Advertising, Brian Henry remembers Roger Kemp's call.

"He used three words: 'We got him.'"

BACK IN LITCHFIELD, Connecticut State Police Detective Karoline Keith submitted an arrest warrant application to State's Attorney John Connolly charging Appleby as a fugitive from justice. The warrant was reviewed and signed by Connolly and then by Superior Court Judge Robert A. Lannotti, confirming the bond at $1 million. At 11 a.m. the same day, while Appleby was in the custody of the Connecticut State Marshals awaiting arraignment, Keith served him the fugitive-from-justice arrest warrant. Keith also advised him of his constitutional rights.

On the afternoon of November 9, Appleby was arraigned. He formally waived his right to contest extradition to Kansas. Senior

State's Attorney John Davenport consulted with the victim in the 1997 indecent exposure case and those charges against Appleby were dismissed. To protect the victim in that crime, the court sealed the case documents.

"What the Connecticut guys did for us," Joe Langer says, "we can never repay. When Scott Hansen called them, they didn't know him from Adam and he didn't know them. I cannot imagine anything more they could have done."

O N NOVEMBER 10, A WEDNESDAY, Roger Kemp went with Brian Henry and Craig Sarver to the billboard on Truman Road in Kansas City, Missouri. There, across the composite illustration of the suspect's face — Benjamin Appleby's face — they placed a banner reading "Captured".

"I had a lump in my throat," Sarver recalls. "The Kemp family had a long way to go, but at least there was some measure of relief in that we were taking Appleby off the streets."

O N NOVEMBER 17, 2004, NINE DAYS AFTER Appleby's confession, Leawood policemen Rodman Lasley and David Winders and Johnson County Deputy Sheriff Brent Moore flew to Connecticut to bring Appleby back to Kansas. All three were specialists in prisoner security. Lasley had met Appleby before, when he took down the name and number of Teddy Hoover at the Foxborough pool on the day Ali Kemp died.

After an extradition hearing in Waterbury Superior Court, Appleby was turned over. He showed no emotion as he rode in an unmarked Connecticut State Police squad car to the airport in Hartford. Moore and Lasley rode with Appleby, and Winders was in a second unmarked State Police vehicle. It was early evening when the three officers and Appleby, in handcuffs, and wearing jeans and a black T-shirt, boarded the Northwest Airlines flight. They entered the plane well before the rest of the passengers and sat in the last row. Appleby sat next to a window.

On the leg from Hartford to Detroit, Moore sat next to him. For a time, Appleby was quiet.

Later in the flight he asked Moore about booking and what

would happen to him once he was back in Kansas City. There would be an arrest report, photographs and fingerprinting. Appleby listened and was quiet for a while. Suddenly, as he looked out the window, Moore recalls, Appleby "made reference to the point that he just lost it." Moore knew what he meant but said nothing in response. Appleby was quiet again for a long time and then told Moore, "Well, at least now her family can have some closure."

Changing flights in Detroit, the group ate dinner at the airport. At one point, out of the blue, Appleby said, "I am going to have to pay for what I have done."

Deputy Moore did not press him to say anything more. On the flight from Detroit to Kansas City, Winders sat next to Appleby. Sometime during that flight Appleby looked at Winders and asked whether he knew the kind of penalties Kansas had for what he had done. Winders said his job was strictly to return Appleby to Johnson County; he should ask either detectives or his attorney. Later in the trip, Appleby engaged in small talk about cleaning swimming pools, and about Lara Barr. And then they were home.

9

Justice

*"Ladies and gentlemen of the jury, it is time
to hold him accountable."*
— Paul Morrison, Johnson County District Attorney

It was already dark on the evening of November 17, 2004, when Benjamin Appleby arrived at Kansas City International Airport. Local reporters and photographers were there, along with a crew from "America's Most Wanted," as detectives escorted Appleby off the plane. Wearing handcuffs and leg irons, he looked frightened and exhausted and stared straight ahead as he was led to squad cars parked on the tarmac.

At that point, Appleby was officially transferred to the custody of the Johnson County Sheriff's Department and driven nearly 40 miles south to the Johnson County Detention Center in Olathe, Kansas.

"When we know that somebody high profile like Appleby was coming," says Sergeant Randy McIntire, "we usually don't mix them with other inmates. People in jail, in institutions, who have allegedly murdered women or children or are sex offenders are looked down upon."

For a while, Appleby was kept in a small, windowless concrete cell. Then he was transferred to another county lockup where, sheriff's deputies said, inmates can be put on a suicide watch. Appleby was dressed in a green "suicide" smock, given only a green blanket in his module and monitored 24 hours a day. After eight days, mental health officials determined that he was not imminently suicidal and he was transferred back to the Johnson County Detention Center. There, he remained in his cell 21 to 23 hours a day.

At 6:30 a.m. every day, a small door in the door of Appleby's cell was unlocked, and breakfast was passed through to him on a metal tray. Then the small door was locked again; he could eat only in his cell. The same procedure was followed for lunch at 11:30 a.m. and dinner at 4:30 p.m. During the day he was allowed out of his cell for one to three hours. Eventually, he was allowed to be around other inmates while he was out of his cell, although no more than two of them. Mostly, he preferred to be alone.

On November 18, the Johnson County prosecutor's office charged Appleby with capital murder and the attempted rape of Ali Kemp. The charges were read to him over closed-circuit television; Appleby remained in jail. He wore a suicide vest.

On December 3 he was taken to the sheriff's property room, where he dressed in a coat and tie. Then he was escorted by deputies through a tunnel underneath Kansas Avenue to the Johnson County Courthouse and the courtroom of Judge Steve Leben of the 10th Judicial District. Security was tight.

Major Craig Hill and Roger Kemp went together to the hearing.

"The horror was there in full focus," Hill recalls. "It is impossible to imagine that such a person as Benjamin Appleby, an absolute predator, actually exists in this world."

Because of the horrific nature of the crime, Hill said, he had visualized Ali Kemp's killer as a monster. Yet he didn't look that way.

"He didn't look terrifying; he looked like the average Joe," Hill recalls. "He was just a punk, but he was a person that had no morals, he had no values, he had no remorse whatever for what he had done. That was immediately obvious."

Appleby looked straight ahead the entire time. The suspect told the judge that he was not going to hire his own attorney. Ronald F. Evans, head of the Kansas Death Penalty Defense Unit, was appointed to represent Appleby.

That day, Roger Kemp saw Appleby in person for the first time.

"When Appleby was brought into the courtroom," Hill recalls,

"Roger never took his eyes off of him."

Kemp remembers focusing on Appleby's face and thinking, "How in God's name could you have done what you did to Ali, our little girl?"

O N DECEMBER 4, 2004, JOHN WALSH and an "America's Most Wanted" crew arrived in Kansas City. That night they honored the army of community volunteers, crime scene investigators, TIPS Hotline personnel and employees of Lamar Outdoor Advertising. John Walsh presented an award to Hill for his relentless commitment to the case. In turn, Leawood Police presented an award to Walsh and crew for their work in helping capture Benjamin Appleby. Words could not express his gratitude, Roger Kemp said.

Through the darkest moments, Kemp added, he had to remind himself that the world was 99.9 percent good.

On December 6 the Leawood City Council adopted a resolution recognizing the work of detectives Hill, Hansen, Langer, Dickey and Hulsey. The next month, the Crime Stoppers staffers who took the important tips, Mike West and Linda Brewer, were honored at a Crime Stoppers breakfast.

Barely a month after Benjamin Appleby's arrest, Sergeant Craig Sarver appeared before the 40 members of the Greater Kansas City Crime Stoppers Board of Directors. He described the leads that made possible the arrest of Benjamin Appleby and recommended how the $50,000 in reward money should be distributed. It was decided that the individual who provided the first tip, in February 2003, would get $10,000. The individual who provided the more detailed second tip, in November 2003, would get $40,000. It would be the largest amount ever awarded to one person by the Kansas City Metropolitan Crime Commission.

Using a code number assigned when the tip was received, Sarver contacted both sources the next day and told them of the awards. The person awarded $10,000 said it was like a gift from God, and would help overcome some severe business difficulties. The recipient was told to write the original code and a second code number on a piece of paper, and then go at a specific time to a specific Kansas City-area bank and give a teller the two codes. The teller would know it was a Crime Stoppers' transaction, but not what case was involved.

When the recipient showed up, the teller took the piece of paper to Sarver and a Crime Stoppers Board member, who were in the bank. Neither could see the recipient, nor could the recipient see them. They verified that the code was correct, gave the tax-free $10,000 in cash to the teller, who in turn handed the award to the recipient. The person's name will never be revealed.

The person eligible for the $40,000 award turned it over to The Ali Kemp Educational Foundation. To take it, the recipient told Sarver, would be like taking blood money.

NEXT CAME MONTHS OF LEGAL WRANGLING. Appleby's court-appointed lawyers argued that his confession had been coerced and that his preliminary hearing ought to be closed to the public. Judge Leben disagreed on both matters, and on September 28, 2005, the preliminary hearing began.

On the second day, Appleby's 19-minute videotaped confession was played in the courtroom. Roger Kemp, sitting only a few feet away from Appleby, heard firsthand how his daughter was killed.

"It was completely devastating," Kemp said, "to learn how she suffered at the hands of this predator."

For his part, Appleby reflected no emotion.

Preliminary hearings determine whether the prosecution has enough evidence to proceed with trial. The judge determined it had.

At his arraignment one month later, Appleby pleaded not guilty. He also argued that he was not receiving acceptable representation from Ronald Evans. Co-counsel Angela Keck took charge of Appleby's defense. She would be assisted by Sarah Swain.

On November 2, District Attorney Paul Morrison of Johnson County announced that he would not seek the death penalty. To meet the restrictive criteria for the death penalty in Kansas, he said, the crime must include at least one of several aggravating factors. The death penalty could be imposed if the crime was committed to avoid or prevent arrest, if the criminal was imprisoned for another felony or had hired another person to commit the homicide, if the criminal committed the crime for pay, if the defendant killed more than one person or had previously committed a crime of great bodily harm or death in another person, or if the victim had been killed as a witness in a criminal proceeding, or in a particularly gruesome manner.

The one potentially aggravating factor in the Ali Kemp case, Morrison said, was the cruelty of the crime. Yet he worried that appellate courts generally interpreted that to mean a victim had been tortured or mutilated or made aware in advance that they were to be killed. That was not the case in this homicide, Morrison said. Also, he noted that two-thirds of all death-penalty convictions nationwide were overturned on appeal. This case, he said, was in line with the standard for capital murder. His plan was to find Appleby guilty and to imprison him for the rest of his life.

Morrison discussed the matter with Roger Kemp, and Kemp disagreed sharply with the decision. Kemp was disappointed, but the matter was out of his control.

"I would like to see Appleby put to death," he said. "I cannot help but feel that we let her down."

O N NOVEMBER 27, 2006 — A YEAR SINCE Benjamin Appleby's arraignment, two years since he was brought back to Kansas and more than four years since the death of Ali Kemp — his trial got under way.

In three days, a jury of 12 persons and three alternates was culled from 105 Johnson County residents summoned for jury duty.

The prosecution began with District Attorney Morrison, who outlined the events of June 18, 2002, and the investigation afterward. Laboratory experts, he said, would testify that the chance of DNA samples from the blood found at the crime scene being from someone other than Benjamin Appleby was one in 14 billion. The prosecution, he continued, would prove that the defendant intentionally killed Ali Kemp "during the course of the commission of the crime of attempted rape."

Morrison concluded, "When the evidence is in, in this case, there will be no doubt that this man killed Ali Kemp, that he did so intentionally."

When the defense's turn came, attorney Angela Keck stunned the courtroom with her opening statement:

"Ladies and gentlemen, this is not a case of whodunit. Mr. Appleby gave a statement to the police. He told them exactly what happened. He was remorseful. We are not asking you to let him go home after this."

Instead, aiming for a lighter punishment, the defense would argue that Appleby had not intended to kill Ali Kemp before he did it. When Appleby blocked her path out of the pump room and Ali Kemp hit him, Keck said, Appleby lost his temper.

He did not remember strangling her, she continued, and would say, "I did not have the intention of doing this. I went in there and lost it and got out of control. I don't know why."

In a "moment of clarity," Keck said, he stopped the attack. He thought Ali was OK and covered her with a tarp. The prosecution had to prove that there was an intent to kill and "premeditation beyond a reasonable doubt."

If Appleby had intended to kill Ali, Keck said, he would not have stopped.

"The only issue you have to decide," Keck told the jury was this: "Has the state proven to you beyond a reasonable doubt that this was an intentional and premeditated murder, and common sense will tell you it is not."

The prosecution called a long series of witnesses. It began with Ali's boyfriend, Phil Howes, who worked the early shift at the pool the day she died, and continued with Ali's friend Laurel Vine, who saw Appleby leave the pool, and then with the Leawood residents who had gone to the pool that afternoon. Ali's brother, Tyler Kemp, told how he became worried when he did not see her at the pool, and Roger Kemp told about finding her in the pump room.

One after another the witnesses appeared: Dispatcher Sarah Reed, who took the 911 call from Roger Kemp, policemen who came to the pool, the firemen who tried in vain to revive Ali Kemp, crime-scene investigators. Leawood policewoman Dianna Johnson told how she had helped with the preliminary examination of Ali's injuries, and how in 2001 she had taken the name and cell phone number of Teddy Hoover after an auto wreck — evidence that helped Leawood police focus on the suspect.

The Johnson County deputy coroner, Michael Handler, described the autopsy. Multiple injuries, Handler said, occurred at virtually the same time to her head, torso and extremities. Death was caused, he said, by the "cumulative effect" of an extraordinary number of severe blunt-force injuries and strangulation. He did not think that the blunt-force injuries alone caused her death; the strangulation may have taken up to 14 minutes.

Witness after witness was called — crime lab personnel, Leawood detectives Ron Hulsey, Scott Hansen, Joseph Langer and John Dickey, and Connecticut detectives David DelVecchia, Daniel Jewiss and Raymond Insalaco.

Then District Attorney Morrison said, "Judge, state rests."

Appleby attorney Keck told Leben that she planned to call one witness the next morning. But at 9 a.m. December 1, the seventh day of the trial, she announced to the court that the defense would have no witness after all, and that the defense rested.

Leben asked Appleby, who was seated between his attorneys, whether he had decided — after consulting with them and as was his Constitutional right — not to testify.

Appleby replied, "I have agreed not to testify."

With that, the judge gave the jury its instruction. Its only concern, he said, was whether Benjamin Appleby was guilty or not guilty of the crimes alleged. The defendant has been "charged with the crimes of capital murder and attempted rape."

The jury could find Appleby guilty of capital murder, first-degree murder, second-degree murder — or not guilty. The offense of capital murder includes "the lesser offense of first-degree murder." In order to establish first-degree murder, he told them, the jury must find that the defendant acted intentionally. In that context, premeditation would mean that Benjamin Appleby thought the matter over before committing the act, but premeditation does not necessarily have to be present before committing an assault.

"Indeed," Leben said, "premeditation can occur at any time during a violent episode that ultimately causes the victim's death."

As for the second charge, the jury must decide between the

charges of attempted rape or completed rape without the consent of the victim.

Morrison began the state's closing argument, saying the crime "was fueled by rage and by sex."

"Benjamin Appleby says he doesn't want anybody to feel sorry for him," Morrison said. "He says he wants to be held accountable. Ladies and gentlemen, it is time to hold him accountable for what he did."

For the defense, Sarah Swain told the jury it was their job to decide what was in Benjamin Appleby's mind when he walked into the pump room. Until Ali hit Appleby, she said, "there is no reflection prior to that. There is no plan. There is no intent. There is no motive. There is nothing."

After the attack, she maintained, "Mr. Appleby went out to his truck and came back to check on Ms. Kemp."

In the second portion of his closing argument, Morrison said the case focused simply on "the deliberate, premeditated beating and murder of an innocent girl."

"You think about the decision that he made and whether or not he committed the overt acts at some point when she rejected him in the dark room," Morrison said, when Appleby said to himself, "I want her, I want sex with her." Appleby, he continued, decided he would take it any way he could get it and, if that was Appleby's premeditated motive, then "you will convict him of capital murder."

The arguments were done by noon on December 5. The jury deliberated until about 3 p.m. When it was announced that the jury was coming back, visitors came in again. Every seat was taken. People were soon standing in rows around the gallery. There was no conversation.

At 3:15 p.m., the jurors filed in to the courtroom. For what seemed like several minutes, the room remained silent; lawyers, family, friends, news media and detectives who had been involved with the case waited.

Judge Leben entered the courtroom. The presiding juror handed the completed verdict forms to the judge's assistant, who handed them to the judge. Leben read the form carefully, looked up, paused and read the verdicts.

The jury, he said, had found Benjamin Appleby guilty on both counts, capital murder and attempted rape.

His sentencing was scheduled for December 26.

A T FIRST, APPLEBY REFUSED TO ATTEND HIS SENTENCING. Then he relented. Deputies took him to the property room, where he put on a coat and tie, and escorted him across the street to the jury room on the eighth floor of the Johnson County Courthouse, adjacent to Leben's courtroom.

That was as far as Appleby would go. The judge was told that he refused to enter the courtroom and also that deputies were concerned about Appleby's mental state that day and whether he would remain calm.

The judge and attorneys talked with Appleby in the jury room as sheriff's deputies stood by.

"I don't want anything to happen in the courtroom," Appleby said, "I don't want to disrespect the court. I don't want anything to happen."

He paused and said, "I was informed that if I was to get out of hand, there is about 10 deputies out there and if I was — needed to be subdued or tied down in some way, which is the way it would have to go down."

He claimed that he had given no indication to anyone that he would be violent in the courtroom.

"But my understanding," Judge Leben replied, "is that you are saying you are concerned that if you were to sit through the hearing this afternoon..."

Appleby interrupted: "I can tell you that I will not sit quietly and listen to distortions and lies about my criminal past and about this case any longer."

Leben asked Appleby whether he understood what could happen in the courtroom that afternoon — a sentence of 50 years without parole was possible on the capital murder conviction; a sentence up to 228 months on the attempted rape charge was possible. Those sentences could be consecutive; one would be served after the other. Appleby said he understood. The judge asked the defendant whether he knew of any reason the court should not proceed with sentencing. Appleby did not.

Told that if he was not present he could not make a statement, Appleby said he understood.

So without Appleby, the hearing began in the courtroom. Morrison announced that Ali Kemp's parents wanted to speak.

Roger Kemp stood, thought for a moment and then described the great opportunities that had been before his daughter before her life was ended.

By contrast, Appleby's life was "filled with lewd acts, violence, armed robbery, assaults against women and prison time."

And now "he doesn't have the courage to sit here today to hear me tell him he is a sub-human."

"Appleby," he said, "is a disgrace to the human race. My immediate family, my extended family, we want him put away where the sun doesn't shine. I am asking you for the maximum sentence for this predator, this child-killer. We don't want him to hurt another person in the world, so don't ever let him out."

Kathy Kemp told how she had grieved over the loss of her daughter.

"Even though it has been four and a half years since I have seen Ali," she said, "I can't believe it is true, even when I am standing at her grave."

She paused, and then said she could not bear to tell stories about Ali as a child. Holding on to her emotions, she paused, and then continued.

She would never see Ali again, never hear her voice. There would never be another picture of her. In the eighth grade she was voted the nicest girl in class; she played sports, was a student ambassador and a member of the National Honor Society. Ali Kemp would now be 24. Letters arrive from other parents of murdered children. Her grave is decorated with candles at Christmas.

"My life and Roger's life and Tyler's and Drew's have been changed in a horrible way," she said. "No matter what you do today, it can never be fixed. She is never, ever coming back."

Arguing for the maximum sentence, District Attorney Morrison said Ali Kemp "is all about what is right with the world and what is good about people." Conversely, the defendant clearly "stands for what is evil in the world. This is the Benjamin Applebys of this world. He has spent his entire life victimizing other people."

The ultimate horror of this crime and the primary reason it outraged so many people, Morrison said, was that Ali Kemp was a good, innocent, decent and popular person simply trying to do her best to do the right thing and be a reasonable citizen.

Then, he said, she was "just picked out from the herd to be killed. That is exactly what happened to Ali Kemp."

WHAT, THEN, MADE BENJAMIN APPLEBY PART of the evil in the world? The defense called Mary K. Poirier, a specialist in biopsychosocial assessments of defendants.

Appleby grew up, she said, in an environment in which his mother was abused mentally and physically and he was beaten — in one situation with a belt. Cocaine and other drugs were abused in his home, and Appleby learned how to grow marijuana at home. There was prostitution in the home, Poirier said.

His parents were divorced when he was 12, and afterward he lived sometimes with his father and other times with his mother. By age 16 he was basically on his own. He drank but did not use drugs.

David George Hough, a clinical psychologist, met with Appleby twice for psychological interviews and testing. He said Appleby had seen prolonged domestic conflict within his own family, perpetrated largely by his father, starting in elementary school.

Punishment in the home included physical beatings with an open hand, belts and fists; verbal abuse included shaming, ridicule and threats of death. At one point, Hough said, the grandfather threatened to "kill the entire family with a loaded weapon."

The death of his boyhood friend, Teddy Hoover, severely inhibited his ability to be close to other people.

In school, Gough continued, Appleby often fought with teachers and other students; his imprisonment at age 17 was brutalizing.

He often showed "a strong outpouring of rage" far out of

proportion to the provocation, resulting in a virtual "collapse of logical thinking or cognitive mediation."

Appleby's emotional façade, the psychologist said, was "easily punctured." He was easily insulted and easily wounded, making him "vulnerable to explosions."

KECK ASKED THE COURT FOR LENIENCY, acknowledging the beating of Ali Kemp but saying the beating "does not rise to the level of especially heinous, atrocious and cruel."

Appleby himself was a victim, Keck implied; he had been brutalized during most of his life and suffered from "intermittent explosive disorder."

If Appleby suffers from such a disorder with episodes of "outpourings of rage and behavior," Leben asked, how could that possibly be a reason for "a lesser sentence instead of a greater sentence?"

"It shows that he was not necessarily in control of his actions," Keck replied. That day at the Foxborough pool, she said, he had a "moment of clarity and he stopped what he was doing," regained some measure of self-control and that "shows some compassion."

Morrison immediately responded, "I think you would be hard pressed, judge, no matter how much research you do, to find a better case than this one" for a strong sentence.

Late in the afternoon, after a short recess, Leben returned to the courtroom. One thousand six hundred fifty days had passed since the horrible events at the Foxborough pool.

In this case, he said, there was "only one living witness to the killing" — Benjamin Appleby. The judge said he had little doubt that Appleby "committed a vicious murder and he has tried in his statement to minimize much of his conduct." The judge stopped, looked up and then recounted events of that day — Appleby said he tried to have sex with Ali Kemp while he was attacking her; Appleby said he panicked; he reacted to being hit by a woman; he said he did not remember strangling her.

The other source of information about what happened in the pump room that day, the judge said, is "Dr. Michael Handler, who performed the autopsy in this case." Leben said that Appleby subjected Ali Kemp to a savage beating; it took up to 16 minutes to strangle her; the strangulation was not continuous, but she was almost dead in the pump room.

"Based upon all the findings set forth here," Leben said, "I conclude that the murder was committed in an especially heinous, atrocious or cruel manner," and it seemed certain that "continuous acts of violence here clearly were committed while the victim was conscious," and further, "he (Appleby) covered her body and closed the door to the pump room to keep her body from being discovered while he left the area."

The judge paused and looked up; the courtroom was silent. Then he spoke again. The law, he said "provides that continuous acts of violence begun before or continuing after the killing by themselves may be considered sufficient evidence that a crime was committed in an especially heinous, atrocious or cruel manner." Additionally, he said, "the same statute provides that the infliction of mental anguish or physical abuse before the victim's death by itself may be considered sufficient for that purpose." The statute's subsections, he added, have "been met by the facts of this case."

"In my view, he should not leave prison." Leben continued. "He represents such a danger to the community that I cannot say that it would ever be appropriate for him to be free."

And so Benjamin Appleby was sentenced to life in prison for capital murder. He would not be eligible for parole for 50 years under Kansas' "Hard 50" sentencing law.

On the attempted rape charge, Appleby was sentenced to 228 months in prison. That sentence would not be served "until the defendant is first paroled on the capital murder sentence. It will be consecutive."

BENJAMIN APPLEBY SPENT 776 DAYS in an 8 x 10-foot maximum security cell, Number 15, on the second floor at the Johnson County Detention Center. A window on one side allowed him to see Santa Fe Street and the railroad tracks that run through downtown Olathe.

While in jail, he was cited nine times for behavioral problems. In one fight, another prisoner lost a finger in a prison door.

"He didn't start the fight," Randy McIntyre of the Sheriff's Department said, "but he finished it."

His fiancée, Lara Barr, visited Appleby during the early part of his Johnson County confinement and again near the end.

After sentencing, Deputy Alan Harris recalls, "Appleby's confidence that he always portrayed was gone. It was the first time I saw the real look of fear in his face. He knew he was going to prison for the rest of his life."

On January 2, 2007, Appleby was ordered to the El Dorado Correctional Facility in El Dorado, Kansas. It is a maximum-security prison and contains the Kansas Department of Corrections Reception and Diagnostic Unit, which processes every inmate received into the custody of the state Department of Corrections.

On his first day, he was assigned an identification number and ID badge, fingerprinted and photographed. Over the next several days, he took extensive medical and psychological tests. On the seventh day, his paperwork was completed.

Then he was transferred to the Kansas State Prison in Lansing.

10

Be Not Overcome of Evil, but Overcome Evil with Good

Romans XII, 21.

"Billboards became right away a new public service weapon for us in the fight against crime. Roger Kemp has become one of my heroes."
— John Walsh, "America's Most Wanted"

"I tell them in self-defense class; if you think this cannot happen to you, just turn our instruction book over. Ali's picture is on the back cover."
— Jill Leiker, self-defense trainer

Ali Kemp's murderer was found, captured, tried, convicted, sentenced and sent to prison. By early 2007, justice had been served.

Today, the public good continues to be served. The search for Ali's killer through a billboard campaign created a brilliant new crime-fighting tool from what had been an everyday sight for millions of motorists across the country.

The Ali Kemp Education Foundation, meanwhile, is spreading the word of women's self-defense nationwide in an effort to reduce the chance that other women will suffer as Ali Kemp did.

THE BILLBOARDS USED TO FIND ALI KEMP'S KILLER went up in February 2003 and remained in view for 19 months. Every day, tens of thousands of drivers along Kansas City-area highways saw the suspect's face and truck and Crime Stoppers TIPS Hotline number. It was an unrelenting effort, virtually unmatched in similar criminal investigations, and it brought to the hotline about 3,000 leads. Among them were leads that led to the arrest of Benjamin Appleby.

Over time, images of other dangerous felons appeared on Kansas City-area billboards. Roger Kemp knew that Crime Stoppers had "stacks" of other fugitives. He worked with Lamar Outdoor Advertising and Kansas City Councilman Alvin Brooks and his Move UP organization, which worked against crime and drug abuse, to set standards for billboard publicity. They would be posted for murders in which a warrant had been issued and a photo of a suspect was available.

"We picked a spot on 71 highway in south Kansas City," Bob Fessler of Lamar says. "We dedicated that very high-traffic billboard to the search for fugitives on a permanent basis. The boards are a great tool, especially when investigators know who the criminal is and they have a photo."

On the final "America's Most Wanted" telecast featuring the Ali Kemp investigation, December 3, 2005, John Walsh pointed to the exceptional ability of billboards to generate leads. Since February 2004 in Kansas City alone, Walsh had learned, eight fugitives whose faces had been posted on 10 Lamar Outdoor billboards had been captured. Seven of the captures, according to Craig Sarver of Crime Stoppers, could be linked directly to tips from the billboards.

"Roger Kemp came up with an absolutely remarkable idea," Walsh says. "I saw how incredibly effective it was in Kansas City. I knew that billboards would immediately increase the effectiveness of 'American's Most Wanted.' Billboards became right away a new public service weapon for us in the fight against crime. Roger Kemp has become one of my heroes."

"America's Most Wanted" went to work with the Outdoor Advertising Association of America, and in May 2005 posted a billboard in Detroit donated by Viacom Outdoor. That campaign resulted in the capture of Phillip "Hollywood" Williams, a career criminal with 41 arrests. Since then billboards placed in high-traffic areas and in combination with "America's Most Wanted" telecasts have become standard operating procedure for the television program.

The advent of digital billboard technology by Daktronics in 2007 in selected markets improved the efficiency and capability of posting fugitive billboards. With digital billboards, images can cycle through every few seconds. As a result, law enforcement can quickly display one or more fugitive messages on one sign. Billboard operators can change fugitive photographs and breaking news at a moment's notice. Billboard messages can be overridden quickly to show alerts for missing children and Alzheimer's patients, and in other emergences.

Lamar's Fessler recalls early 2007, when the billboard industry was starting to put up the electronic devices.

"All of a sudden," Fessler says, "people started thinking, Wow, the digital billboard would be perfect for this format."

That same year, "America's Most Wanted" telecasts ran in combination with wanted billboards in Phoenix, Dallas, Atlanta, Cincinnati, New York, Milwaukee, Indianapolis, Charlotte, Philadelphia and Wichita, Kansas.

After a jail break in Yakima County, Washington, police put photos of two escapees on a high-traffic thoroughfare billboard. Both were apprehended within a month.

In Passaic, New Jersey, multiple billboards helped police capture a suspect in the stabbing death of a policeman's son.

In Philadelphia, photos of 11 of the city's most violent fugitives were posted on eight billboards donated by Clear Channel Holdings. Targeted criminals were selected by FBI special agents and police detectives.

A Crime Stoppers-funded billboard campaign in the Columbus, Georgia, area led to the apprehension of Raymond Leon Richmond, wanted for probation violation, six counts of aggravated assault, third-degree cruelty to children, battery with physical harm, simple battery and illegal use of a firearm.

A few months later in Dallas, a suspect wanted for murder, attempted murder and aggravated robbery turned himself in two weeks after his photo was posted on billboards.

In Mobile, Alabama, a man wanted in a bank robbery, Oscar

Finch, saw billboards showing his face. He called his pastor, who notified police. Mobile law enforcement agencies can flash photos and names of suspects or missing people on 13 digital billboards in the Mobile area within minutes of a police report. Billboards also are used in cases of abducted children or missing Alzheimer patients, when time is crucial.

"This one element could be the lifeline for some of our most vulnerable citizens," Mobile Police Chief Phillip Garret says.

In February 2008, the FBI kicked off the bureau's first digital billboard campaign to search for top fugitives in bank robberies, kidnappings and other crimes. It covered 20 cities — Akron, Albuquerque, Atlanta, Chicago, Cleveland, Columbus, Des Moines, El Paso, Indianapolis, Las Vegas, Los Angles, Memphis, Miami, Milwaukee, Minneapolis, Newark, Orlando, Philadelphia, Tampa and Wichita. In the campaign the FBI accessed about 150 electronic billboards, all donated by Clear Channel Outdoor Holdings Inc. The FBI counts at least eight apprehensions directly from publicity from the billboards.

From Tampa, Florida, to Janesville, Wisconsin, police have found billboards an enormous aid not only in catching criminals but also in tracking down Alzheimer's sufferers

In spring 2008 in Hattiesburg, Mississippi, a 16-year-old girl was viciously raped. A car chase of the suspect failed, but the Marion County Sheriff's office put the suspect's image on television and on an electronic billboard on U.S. 98 in Hattiesburg. Within minutes phone tips came in that led police to the suspect.

In Milwaukee six billboards were donated to help police investigate a July 4 quadruple homicide involving local drug traffic. By July 16, one of the suspects had been captured. Photos of two more mob suspects were featured every four minutes on six billboards. Motorists were urged to call police with the message, "It's Gut-Check Time. Take Back Your Neighborhood."

In less than a generation, the use of billboards in criminal investigations since the first posting in Kansas City in early 2003 has spread to scores of cities across the country. As Ken Kline of the Outdoor Advertising Association of America notes, "we see the day when billboard usage will be standard operating procedure in almost all police jurisdictions. It makes us wonder why the idea had never been thought of before. The credit, of course, goes to Roger Kemp."

IN LATE 2003, WHILE THE SEARCH FOR THEIR daughter's killer was still grinding on, Roger and Kathy Kemp met with officials at the Johnson County Parks and Recreation District. They wanted to establish, as a test project, a program of self-defense classes for women.

Parks and Recreation agreed and chose Jill Leiker, a recreation specialist with the district, to direct it. She has a black belt in karate and 20 years' experience teaching self-defense.

In January 2004 she held the first class for 20 women. The program was fine-tuned and classes were made available in three parks and recreation districts: Johnson County, Blue Valley and Leawood. In a few weeks, the program had a waiting list of 368 women.

Leiker had hoped to limit enrollment size to 20 women per class so she could work individually with each. From the first month, however, demand was so great and classes so large that more instructors were added.

"We basically tripled our offering," she says.

Then as now, the goal was to provide women 12 and older skills to avoid being victims of violent crime.

"I tell women before each class," Leiker says, "if you think that something violent cannot happen to you, please, right now, turn your instruction book over. Ali Kemp's picture is on the back cover.

"There is no way in the world that anyone would think this would happen to Ali and this is why you should know this could happen to you."

Participants are encouraged to bring a friend. Mother-and-daughter teams work well. The first hour of each two-hour session teaches safety awareness and the second hour physical defense techniques. There is one goal: to save their lives.

A primary message is to change unsafe behavior.

"I hope," Leiker says, "that a woman is never in a situation where she has to fight back. I hope that she has learned in the class to not find herself in a bad situation."

The training encourages women to be constantly aware of their surroundings; if some situation or surrounding feels wrong, something probably is wrong, and it's better to be safe than sorry.

In each class, women face a simulated attack and practice responding to it.

A potential assailant, participants are told, has no regard for them as a woman or as a human being. An assailant could be out there right now, trying to figure out how to make a woman, any woman, a victim. It might be his full-time obsession. An assailant is intent on getting what he wants, in any way possible, without regard for a woman's family, friends, or her life. An assailant will not hesitate to inflict physical damage even if, as in the case of Ali Kemp, the assault leads to death.

What to do? For one, instructors say, criminals don't like sound because it draws attention. Sound is a victim's friend; it can buy time. Participants are encouraged to scream, yell and hit hard and fast, and to make every effort to get away. A victim fighting back with all her resources creates surprise, which can save her life.

Assailants often attack quickly, and they don't have a lot of time. A noisy, furious response may tell an attacker that the assault is not worth the effort.

Fear and adrenaline, women are taught, can be extraordinary sources of power — with proper training.

Predators and misfits are always looking for easy targets, the instructors say. They loiter in grocery stores, malls, convenience stores and parking lots — almost anywhere a woman may be alone.

The average predator observes his potential victim six to 12 times before attacking. He will get close to the potential victim once or twice to boost his confidence. He may exhibit warning signs such as rapid eye movement, frequent clenching of his fists, unusual and often broken speech patterns and excessive perspiration on his forehead or palms.

Four out of five potential assaults can be stopped, participants are told, if a woman sets boundaries through powerful and well-directed words.

Instructors categorize three levels of threat.

Yellow Alert describes the first awareness that something isn't right. In response, a woman should establish her protective space with words or by putting up her hands. That sends a message to a potential assailant: You're too close, and I am uncomfortable about it. Simply letting a potential assailant know he has been seen can deter him.

Orange Alert represents a heightened awareness of potential danger. More assertive words — telling the man to back off or leave — are necessary.

At Red Alert, words have failed and the assailant is not going away. The woman must become loud in telling the man to leave and prepare to use adrenaline, fear and training to protect herself. She must fight until she can escape to safety, and then contact police immediately.

"We are not talking about standing toe to toe with a man 6-2, 240 pounds and trying to fight him off," Jill Leiker says. "Hit one of four vital targets — eyes, nose, throat, groin — and get away. It's that simple."

Participants in the program are provided a handbook for reference after they complete the program. Each woman also receives a certificate and large color poster with the caption, "Find out why fighting like a girl can be a good thing."

BY LATE 2004, The Ali Kemp Educational Foundation had more than $100,000 in funds — about half from individual donors, 40 percent from corporate donations and 10 percent from associations and other organizations. Some was used for $1,000 college scholarships for 11 high school students, another role of the foundation. Meanwhile, it financed expanded self-defense programs for women and established a website, www.takedefense.org.

In fall 2004 the program trained 150 sorority women at the University of Kansas.

"That was the first time we had trained a class of that size," Jill Leiker said, "the group dynamics of that many people doing exactly the same training in one huge gymnasium was amazing."

In March 2005, eight instructors traveled to Vanderbilt University in Nashville, Tennessee, to do a training session organized with the assistance of the Panhellenic Council. Women packed the student recreation center.

On March 5, 2005, ABC News "Primetime Live" taped a T.A.K.E. self-defense class for 110 women at Heartland Elementary School in Overland Park, Kansas. Part of a December 2005, "America's Most Wanted" program focused on the T.A.K.E self-defense classes. Production director David Bolton noticed how women entering the class appeared timid and unassuming, not knowing what to expect.

"When they left here," he said, "they were empowered. They were completely different people."

T.A.K.E. self-defense classes were presented at the University of Missouri-Kansas City, the College of New Jersey and Rutgers University. Ali Kemp's affiliation with the Pi Beta Phi sorority at Kansas State introduced the T.A.K.E. program to chapters nationwide and in turn to other sororities.

The program expanded every month and by summer 2008, 25,000 women had received training, ranging from middle-school students to an 86-year-old. Foundation planners try to maintain the integrity of the program, honor the memory of Ali Kemp, and continue to reach out.

At least one in 20 participants, says Jill Leiker, has been subject to a violent incident or traumatized in some other way by a predator.

"It is astonishing how many women tell their stories to us after the class," she reports. "We are seeing a change in their attitudes. They want to share it. It is not a secret any more."

Leiker now incorporates some of those stories, without names, in the curriculum.

One woman came out of a grocery store, walked across the parking lot on a sunny afternoon, got into her car and was confronted by an unknown armed man in the back seat.

Another woman arrived home in late afternoon, closed her garage door, went inside to fix dinner and suddenly found a man she did not know standing in her kitchen, waiting to assault her.

"We talk about car-jackings in which women have been violently assaulted," Leiker says, "or what happened to a woman when a man somehow gained entrance to her house and climbed into her bed at 2 in the morning. She was assaulted."

After class, a woman told Leiker how a member of her family began assaulting her when she was 12 years old and continued assaulting her for years. The woman had thought, even as an adult, that if she was ever approached she would simply submit because there was nothing she could do. The self-defense class, she told Leiker tearfully, had taught her that she did not have to submit to unwanted advances and physically could now resist.

Besides teaching classes, the foundation staff certifies new trainers. The aim, Leiker says, is to build a training network across the country. With qualified and committed trainers at various places, live, on-line training will be possible through video teleconferencing from Kansas City. Sessions can take place anywhere in the country at the same time, all at no cost.

"We want to train women as well as we possibly can," Roger Kemp says, "because the quality and absolute integrity of the Ali Kemp program is crucial. We can never lose that."

The foundation plans to build a new video and administrative center in the Kansas City area. It aims to use fundraising to pay operating costs through 2011. The foundation's continuing marketing plan is to attract new corporate partners, individual partners and students through direct mail advertising, e-mail promotions, the organization's website, fashion shows and continuing media exposure.

There is no similar program anywhere in the world; what makes the Ali Kemp program remarkably different is that it's free. Martial arts business may offer an opening session for free, but that's in hopes of attracting paying customers.

As the Kemp family found out, there are few resources in the United States that explain how to set up and organize a self-defense program for women. There are no books on the subject.

Requests for training classes generally arrive at the foundation through the T.A.K.E. website. Many requests for classes have come from colleges and universities.

In colleges, Leiker says, "young people will hear about the Ali Kemp program on their own. Word of mouth is just simply astonishing."

The travel team consists of Jill Leiker, her husband Bob, also a black belt in karate and the class's co-instructor, and Roger Kemp. For every training session, an organizer arranges for a training room with registration tables and a small stage for classes of 200 or more. Classes have been as large as 600.

If the class is within driving distance of the foundation office, life-size manikins are carried in a trailer to use in demonstrations. To serve as many women as possible, class sizes of at least 100 are preferred.

The two-hour class follows a timeline including segments on awareness and boundary-setting with 45 minutes set aside for "combat exercises."

At the end, students fill out evaluation forms. The completed forms are entered in a database. As the database grows, it provides the foundation a wealth of first-hand sociological information about the safety of women in America.

"Often the group that is organizing the class," Roger Kemp reports, "will invite other groups to the class. They may bring the whole Greek community as well as independent students on campus together at one time."

Members of the college administration are also contacted, and the classes may include women in administration and wives of instructors.

"On many campuses," Roger Kemp says, "this becomes a very significant event."

The ultimate aim?

"In a perfect world, every woman everywhere would be trained in self-defense," Jill Leiker says. "Our goals are high — very high. If we can train 25,000 women by ourselves; imagine what we can do with 25 instructors or 250 instructors!"

Afterword

The story of the Ali Kemp homicide and investigation is a story that must be told. Craig Hill, now retired from the Leawood Police, gives three reasons.

First, the Ali Kemp slaying makes it clear that American children are at risk, no matter where they are and no matter where they live. Crime can strike a young person even in an upscale neighborhood, even in a public place with thousands of people nearby. It can happen there as easily as in a dark alley.

Second, predators are everywhere. As the case of Benjamin Appleby showed, they cannot be identified by appearance. They are in every walk of life.

Third, finding a killer — even against almost unimaginable odds — can succeed through sheer force of will. The investigation of Ali Kemp's murder never ceased, no matter how long it took, until the assailant was brought to justice. This extraordinary investigation called upon the talents of hundreds of people across the United States, each driven by powerful emotions, each working for justice.

The lasting impact of Ali Kemp's death has been profound — the creation of free self-defense programs for women with the ultimate goal of training women throughout the hemisphere, and the introduction of electronic billboard technology in police investigations throughout the United States.

The sadness of losing her will always be with those who knew her and those who knew of her. Ali's legacy is profound, and even though she lived for such a short time, the world is a better place because Ali was here.

Acknowledgments

I am indebted to a number of people of great talent who provided valuable assistance in preparing this book.

First and foremost, I am indebted to Doug Weaver, manager of book publishing and retail merchandising at *The Kansas City Star,* and my editor, Monroe Dodd.

Major Craig Hill, formerly deputy chief of the Leawood Police Department, worked closely on the complex Ali Kemp homicide investigation and authorized the creation of the Major Case Squad the day after the crime. I owe many thanks to him and to Detective Sergeant Scott Hansen, who directed the search for the assailant and maintained the enormous lead files with Unit Secretary Alison Wacker. Hansen and Leawood detectives Joseph Langer, Ron Hulsey and John Dickey worked tirelessly on the investigation and yet made themselves available to provide information on the investigation, for interviews and for critical fact-checks. Officer Dianna Johnson, formerly with the Leawood Police Department and a specialist in gathering forensic evidence from victims of sexual assault, provided me information regarding the initial hospital examination of the victim.

Sergeant Craig Sarver, Kansas City Metro Area Crime Stoppers coordinator, worked directly with Leawood Police and other police enforcement agencies in processing and monitoring several thousand tips and leads generated during the investigation. Sergeant Sarver provided me detailed firsthand information.

I appreciated the opportunity to meet and interview Tom Prudden, a detective with the East Property Crimes Section of the Kansas City Missouri Police Department. Detective Prudden, who served as Public Information Officer for the Major Case Squad, assembled the squad the day after the homicide.

Detectives Daniel Jewiss, Raymond Insalaco and David DelVecchia of the Connecticut Western District Major Case Squad committed the district's resources to the investigation and arrested the assailant in Bantam, Connecticut. These investigators also provided crucial testimony during the Appleby criminal trial in

Kansas. I am thankful for their careful attention to detail regarding the Connecticut portion of the investigation.

Captain Michael Raunig, Operations Bureau commander, Deputy Steven Buehler, courthouse supervisor, deputies Alan Harris and Randy McIntire, and Master Deputy Terry Heathman, all with the Johnson County Sheriff's Department, provided details of Benjamin Appleby's incarceration and courtroom security for the many hearings and the trial.

Allan Hamm, assistant director of the Johnson County Crime Lab, an expert on DNA profiling, read selected chapters of the manuscript, and gave me the benefit of his many years of experience.

I would like to acknowledge the expert assistance of Jill Leiker, a black belt in karate and executive director of the Ali Kemp Foundation. I met with Jill several times and benefited from her considerable knowledge and commitment to the foundation.

My gratitude also goes to Veronica Dersch and Paul Morrison, both previously of the Johnson County District Attorney's Office. I appreciated their review of the text regarding the extensive hearing and jury trial proceedings.

Leawood Mayor Peggy J. Dunn systematically followed developments during the entire 29-month investigation. She congratulated, on behalf of the city, members of the investigative team on the successful conclusion of the investigation. I appreciated the opportunity to interview her and her editing of portions of the text.

The remarkable participation of John Walsh, host of "America's Most Wanted," was critical to the investigation. Many thanks to him for writing the foreword for this book and to Dave Bolton, producer, and Lance Helflin, executive producer of "America's Most Wanted." The program's early participation in the investigation was largely the result of Major Hill's close friendship with John Walsh. Members of the organization reviewed the manuscript.

Bob Fessler, vice president and general manager of Lamar Outdoor Advertising, made the extraordinary decision to use billboards advertising in the Ali Kemp investigation. I appreciated his considerable input and that of Brian Henry, creative director at Lamar. Ken Klein, executive vice president for government relations of the Outdoor Advertising Association of America in Washington, supplied information on the rapid growth of the use of billboards in criminal investigations across the United States.

Lee Hammond, widely known forensic artist based in the Kansas City area, volunteered her time and expertise in creating the composite illustration of the assailant used throughout the investigation. I am particularly thankful for her input regarding the meticulous creative process that resulted in the final illustration of the assailant.

Abby J. Ryan, official court reporter, Division 8, Johnson County Courthouse, made copies of hearing and trial proceedings for me in manageable form.

I appreciate the support of my wife, Neva, and the text suggestions by Mary Rogers-Grantham, consultant for the Greater Kansas City Writing Project at the University of Missouri-Kansas City.

Appendix

"America's Most Wanted" script, August 3, 2002

AUDIO	VIDEO
John Walsh: Good evening. It is the heart of the summer and this pool in the suburbs of Kansas City should be filled with the sounds of splashing and laughter. Instead, it is quiet and closed. Instead, this pool house behind me was the scene of a shocking murder. And the victim was a beautiful young college girl who was full of life. This high school video in which she is making fun of fashion models, Ali Kemp's free spirit shines through. She was young, fun-loving and had a great future.	John is standing in front of the Leawood, Kansas swimming pool pump room where Ali Kemp was killed.
	Ali Kemp high school photos on camera
Kathy Kemp: She had finished her freshman year at K-State and had a fabulous, fabulous year. She did well, joined a sorority and it was the best year of her life. We talked so many times in the last few months. Couldn't believe she was going to be 20 in October. And how old that sounded and she couldn't believe she was going to be 20 years old.	Kathy Kemp on camera
John Walsh: Ali was at home in Leawood, Kansas, on summer break working as an attendant at this community pool. This pool was only a mile away from Ali's home.	John Walsh on camera
Kathy Kemp: Never would we have thought about her being unsafe there. Never.	Kathy Kemp interview
Roger Kemp: She thought she had the best of all possible worlds and she enjoyed it very much and often her friends would stop by to see her. She was very happy.	Roger Kemp interview
John Walsh: But that would change on June 18. It was a cloudy and rainy day and no one was at the pool, or so she thought. Cops say there was someone else at the pool that day. Ali was working inside the pool area and they say a man entered through the front gate.	John Walsh copy
Detective Joe Langer: The suspect encountered the victim, Ali Kemp, who was sitting at a table right here. Somehow he talked the victim into going into the pump room area. Once he had Ali Kemp inside, a fight ensued and she was beaten and her body was placed over in this area of the pump room.	Joe Langer interview
John Walsh: Ali Kemp fought for her life, but she was no match for her attacker. She was dead in a matter of minutes. Cops say the suspect covered Ali with a pool cover and then simply walked away. Not before someone got a really good look at him.	John Walsh copy
Major Hill: At 3:15, one of Ali's girlfriends from school pulled into the parking lot and honked her horn, hoping that Ali would come out and visit with her. And she observed a white man in his mid	Major Hill interview

AUDIO	VIDEO
30s who looked directly at this young lady.	
John Walsh: Ali's friend saw a strange man get into a 1980s beige Ford pickup and take off. She looked around the pool area and when she didn't see Ali, she left. Ali's brother arrived soon after to take over his sister's shift. But when he couldn't find Ali, he called his dad and together they searched the pool area. It was Roger Kemp who went into the pool area and discovered his daughter's body.	Girl driving a car up to pool complex parking lot
Roger Kemp: The first 7 days were the longest days of our lives and it has gotten worse. I don't know how you can ever accept something like this.	Roger Kemp interview
John Walsh: As investigators began piecing things together, they had a few clues. Ali's friend had seen the killer and knew what he looked like. A forensic artist made this sketch based on the friend's memory.	Lee Hammond sketching the composite of suspect.
Lee Hammond: When you meet someone, there is always something that stands out about that person. This individual, she remembered, seemed to have a round face and thick brown hair.	Lee Hammond interview
John Walsh: The cops have not been able to find the man in this sketch and now they are asking for your help. Investigators say the suspect probably works around pool areas. They believe that the man who killed Ali Kemp stalked and targeted her. In fact, after seeing the sketch, witnesses say that they saw him hanging around the pool earlier that day.	Multiple shots of composite and photo of suspects pickup truck.
Kathy Kemp: There is not going to be justice for us because this beautiful, precious person is gone. We don't want this to happen to anyone else.	Kathy Kemp interview
Roger Kemp: He stalked her and went after her, just for the purpose he had of taking her life. This predator has to be caught or he is going to do it again.	Roger Kemp interview
John Walsh: Let's make sure this doesn't happen. Let's get this sick and dangerous man off the streets now. Ali Kemp's killer was last seen in a 1980s beige Ford pick up like this one. Cops say he may be a traveler. He may use this truck for maintenance or handyman work. If you think you've seen the man in this sketch please call 1-800 CRIME TV. This story is absolutely heartbreaking, not only for Ali's family, and I have met her loving dad, but it has also broken the hearts of everyone here in Leawood, Kansas. Let's catch this coward tonight. Remember, this is the show you can call and remain anonymous. And there is a $50,000 reward for this creep's capture. Please do the right thing and make this call.	John Walsh on camera

Notes

Chapter 1: Day of Unreason
Page
2. Roger Kemp, interview with the author, 1 March 2006.
3. Ibid.
4. Ibid.
4. Ben Conery, "Death by the pool," *Republican-American* newspaper, Waterbury, Connecticut, 10 January 2006, pp. 2-3.
4. Richard Espinoza and James Hart, "Metro Squad looks into beating death," *The Kansas City Star*, 20 June 2002, pp. A1-3.
5. Roger Kemp, interview with the author, 1 March 2006.
7. In the District Court of Johnson County, Kansas Criminal Court Department, Jury Trial, Day 3, "Testimony of Laurel Vine," 29 November 2006, p. 99.
8. In the District Court of Johnson County, Kansas, Criminal Court Department, Jury Trial, Day 3, "Testimony of Tamara Baker," 29 November 2006, p. 131.
9. In the District Court of Johnson County, Kansas, Criminal Court Department, Jury Trial, Day 3, "Testimony of Meredith Lindsey," 29 November 2006, p.142.
10. Roger Kemp, interview with the author, 11 March 2006.
10. In the District Court of Johnson County, Kansas, Criminal Court Department, Jury Trial, Day 3, "Testimony of Police Dispatcher Sarah Reed," 29 November 2006, p. 260.
11. In the District Court of Johnson County, Kansas, Criminal Court Department, Jury Trial, Day 4, "Testimony of Firefighter Eric Peterson," 30 November 2006, p. 12.
12. In the District Court of Johnson County, Kansas, Criminal Court Department, Jury Trial, Day 5, "Testimony of Police Officer Rodman Lasley," 1 December 2006, p. 7.
12. In the District Court of Johnson County, Kansas, Criminal Court Department, Jury Trial, Day 3, "Testimony of Laurel Vine," 29 November 2006, p. 106.
13. In the District Court of Johnson County, Kansas, Criminal Court Department, Jury Trial, Day 3, "Testimony of Phil Howes," 29 November 2006, p. 78.
13. Detective Joe Langer, interview with the author, 2 February 2006.

Chapter 2: Benjamin Appleby
Page

16. Ben Conery, "Part I: Escape to Connecticut," *Republican-American,* 10 January 2006, p. 2.
17. Ibid.
17-18. Matt Sedensky, "Murder suspect had local ties," The Associated Press and by *The Examiner* staff, 10 November 2004, pp.1-2.
18. Ben Conery, "Part I: Escape to Connecticut," *Republican-American,* 10 January 2006, p.2.
18-19. In the Circuit Court of Jackson County, Missouri, at Independence, Statement of Probable Cause, 27 June 1992.
19. Ben Conery, "Part I: Escape to Connecticut," *Republican-American,* 10 January 2006, p. 3.
20. Ibid.
20. In the Circuit Court of Jackson County, Missouri, at Independence, Complaint, 8 February 1996.
20-21. Kevin Hoffman, "Records, recollections tell of lives poles apart; Accused was seen as a high risk years ago," *The Kansas City Star,* 11 November 2004, pp.1-2.

Chapter 3: Night of Anguish
Page
23. City of Leawood, Mayor Peggy Dunn, interview with the author, 8 January 2008.
24. In the District Court of Johnson County, Kansas, Criminal Court Division, Jury Trial, Day 4, "Testimony of Johnson County Deputy Corner, Michael Handler," 30 November 2006, pp. 211-212.
24-25. Detective Joe Langer, interview with the author, 2 February 2006.
25. Police Officer Dianna Johnson, interview with the author, 9 April 2006.
25-26. In the District Court of Johnson County, Kansas, Criminal Court Department, Jury Trial, Day 5, "Testimony of Allen Hamm," 1 December 2006, p. 105.
26. In the District Court of Johnson County, Kansas, Criminal Court Department, Jury Trial, Day 4, "Testimony of Lyla Thompson," 30 November 2006, p. 81.
26. In the District Court of Johnson County, Kansas, Criminal Court Department, Jury Trial, Day 3, "Testimony of Laurel Vine," 29 November 2006, p.107.
26. Ibid. p. 101.
27. Roger Kemp, interview with the author, 1 March 2006.

Chapter 4: The Investigation Begins
Page

30. Major Craig Hill, interview with the author, 2 March 2006.

31. Roger Kemp, interview with the author, 1 March 2006.

31. Detective Tom Prudden, interview with the author, 2 February 2006.

33. Lee Hammond, interview with the author, 19 April 2006.

33. Donna McGuire, "Crowd celebrates life of homicide victim," *The Kansas City Star*, 23 June 2002, pp. B1-2.

35. Richard Espinoza and James Hart, "Metro Squad looks into beating death," *The Kansas City Star*, 20 June 2002, p. A1.

36. Richard Espinoza, "Leawood police take charge of Kemp case," *The Kansas City Star*, 29 June 2002, pp. B1-2.

Chapter 5: America's Most Wanted
Page
37. John Walsh with Susan Schindehette, *Tears of Rage* (New York: Pocket Books, Division of Simon & Schuster, 1997). p.112.

37-38. Ibid. p. 289.

39. Roger Kemp, interview with the author, 1 March 2006.

40. Ibid.

41. Ibid.

43. Detective Joe Langer, interview with the author, 29 September 2006.

Chapter 6: New England and Back
Page
45. State of Connecticut, Division of Public Safety, Division of State Police, Witness Statement of Tammy Wyatt, 12 November, 2004.

47. State of Connecticut, New Milford Police Department, Statement of Benjamin Appleby, 16 February 1998.

48. Ben Conery, "Part II: Like 2 different people," *Republican-American*, 9 January 2006.

48. State of Connecticut, New Milford Police Department, Statement of Benjamin Appleby, 16 February 1998.

48. State of Connecticut, Department of Public Safety, Division of State Police, Witness Statement, 8 August 1997.

48-49. Ben Conery, "Part II: Like 2 different people," *Republican-American*, 9 January 2006, p.2.

49. Officer.Com, The Source for Law Enforcement, "Accused Connecticut killer pleaded for help years before strangling," 17 November 2004, pp.1-3.

49.   State of Connecticut, New Milford Police Department, Statement of Benjamin Appleby, 16 February 1998.

49.   Matt Stearns, "Suspects arrest rocks Bantam Road," *The Kansas City Star*, 11 November 2004, pp. 1-5.

50.   Ben Conery, "Part III: Death by the pool," *Republican-American*, 10 January 2006, p. 2.

50.   "Ex-Neighbor talks about Appleby," KCTV5, 10 November 2004.

50-51. Ben Conery, "Part III: Death by the pool," *Republican-American*, 10 January 2006, p. 2.

51.   Tony Rizzo, "Pool suppliers knew Kemp suspect," *The Kansas City Star*, 12 November 2004, p. B1.

51.   Ben Conery, "Part III: Death by the pool," *Republican-American*, 10 January 2006, p.1.

Chapter 7: The Long Search
Page

53.   Detective Sergeant Scott Hansen, interview with the author, 21 February 2006.

54.   Detective Joe Langer, interview with the author, 23 February 2006.

54.   Ben Conery, "Part IV: They're trying to stir up something from my past," *Republican- American*, 11 January 2006, pp. 1-2.

55.   Major Craig Hill, interview with the author, 2 March 2006.

55.   Detective Joe Langer, interview with the author, 23 February 2006.

56-57. Major Craig Hill, interview with the author, 2 March 2006.

57.   Erin Fitzgerald, "Self defense classes to honor area woman's memory: Ali Kemp foundation offering free classes across country," *The Kansas City Star*, 14 August 2004, pp. 1-3.

57.   Erik Petersen, "Kemp scholarship fund swells," *The Kansas City Star*, 9 August 2002, p. B1.

57.   Melodee Hall Blobaum, "Ali delighted, inspired her friends," *The Kansas City Star*, 11 November 2004, pp. B1-B3.

57.   Jeffrey Flanagan, "Royals hope arrest helps bring closure to Kemps," *The Kansas City Star*, 12 November 2004, pp. 1-3.

58.   Detective Sergeant Scott Hansen, interview with the author, 21 February 2006.

58.   Roger Kemp, interview with the author, 1 March 2006.

59.   Roger Kemp, interview with the author, 5 February 2008.

59.   Detective Sergeant Scott Hansen, interview with the author, 21 February 2008.

60.   Major Craig Hill, interview with the author, 3 March 2006.

60.   Roger Kemp, interview with the author, 5 February 2008.

61.   Ibid.

61. Major Craig Hill, interview with the author, 3 March 2006.

61. Bob Fessler, interview with the author, 7 March 2008.

62. Roger Kemp, interview with the author, 5 February 2008.

62. Detective Joe Langer, interview with the author, 29 September 2008.

62. Crime Stoppers of Greater Kansas City, 14 February 2003.

63. Detective John Dickey, interview with the author, 7 October 2006.

63. Detective Joe Langer, interview with the author, 23 February 2006.

64. Roger Kemp, interview with the author, 1 March 2006.

64-65. K. Joseph Langer, Leawood Police Department, Supplemental Report #0655, 9 May 2003.

65. K. Joseph Langer, Leawood Police Department, Supplemental Report, #0703, 19 June 2003.

66. Detective Joe Langer, interview with the author, 29 September 2008.

66-67. Detective Sergeant Scott Hansen, Leawood Police Department, Supplemental Report #1304, 9 September 2003.

67-68. Ben Conery, "Part IV: They're trying to stir up something from my past," *Republican-American*, 11 January 2006, p. 2.

68. Sergeant Craig Sarver, interview with the author, 6 August 2006.

Chapter 8: Closing In
Page
71. Detective Sergeant Scott Hansen, interview with the author, 21 February 2006.

72. Ibid.

73-74. Ibid.

74. Detective John Dickey, interview with the author, 10 July 2006.

75. State of Connecticut, Superior Court, Search and Seizure Warrant, #DPSO4055411, 8 November 2004.

76. In the District Court of Johnson County, Kansas, Criminal Court Department, Motion Hearing, "Testimony of Sergeant David DelVecchia," 11 July 2006 pp. 3-11.

76. Detective Sergeant Scott Hansen, interview with the author, 9 January 2007.

77. State of Connecticut, Department of Public Safety, Narrative Report, submitted by Detective Daniel Jewiss, 8 November 2004.

77-78. In the District Court of Johnson County, Kansas, Criminal Court Department, Preliminary Hearing, Testimony of Detective Raymond Insalaco, 29 September 2005.

78. Detective Sergeant Scott Hansen, interview with the author, 9

January 2007.

79.   Detective Joe Langer, interview with the author, 23 February 2006.
79.   Detective John Dickey, interview with the author, 7 October 2006.
80.   Detective Joe Langer, interview with the author, 23 February 2006.
80.   Detective John Dickey, interview with the author, 7 October 2006.
81.   Detective Joe Langer, interview with the author, 23 February 2006.
81.   Detective John Dickey, interview with the author, 7 October 2006.
83.   Detective Joe Langer, interview with the author, 23 February 2006.
83.   Detective John Dickey, interview with the author, 7 October 2006.
84.   "Homicide suspect's trail led from Kansas to Connecticut,"
       Republican-American, 13 January 2006, p. 6.
84.   Detective Sergeant Scott Hansen, interview with the author, 9
       January 2007.
84.   Alison Wacker, interview with the author, 9 September 2007.
84-85. City of Leawood Mayor Peggy Dunn, interview with the author, 8
       January 2008.
85.   Jill Leiker, interview with the author, 7 May 2008.
85.   Sergeant Craig Sarver, interview with the author, 8 June 2006.
85.   Brian Henry, interview with the author, 12 May 2006.
86.   Detective Joe Langer, interview with the author, 23 February 2006.
86-87. In the District Court of Johnson County, Kansas Criminal Court
       Department, Preliminary Hearing, "Testimony of Deputy Brent
       Moore," 29 September 2005, pp. 453-470.

Chapter 9: Justice
Page
89.   Sergeant Randy McIntyre, Johnson County Sheriff's Department,
       interview with the author, 12 December 2007.
90-91. Major Craig Hill, interview with the author, 2 March 2006.
91.   Roger Kemp, interview with the author, 5 February 2008.
92.   Ibid.
93.   Diane Carroll, "Death won't be sought for Appleby. Father asks:
       'Where's the justice in this?'" *The Kansas City Star*, 3 November
       2005, pp. 1-5.
93-94. In the District Court of Johnson County, Kansas, Criminal Court
       Department, Transcript of Proceedings, Jury Trial, Day 7, 5
       December 2006, p. 27.
94.   Ibid. pp. 29-41.
95.   In the District Court of Johnson County, Kansas, Criminal Court
       Department, Transcript of Proceedings, Jury Trial, Day 7, 5
       December 2006, p. 5.
95-96. Ibid. p. 38.

96.   Ibid. p. 49.
96.   Ibid. p. 59.
96.   Ibid. p. 71.
97.   In the District Court of Johnson County, Kansas, Criminal Court
        Department, Transcript of Proceedings, Sentencing, 26 December
        2006, pp. 18-19.
98.   Ibid. pp. 69-74.
99-100. Ibid. pp. 79, 83-84, 129, 135.
100.   Ibid. pp. 144-145, 149.
101.   Ibid. pp.152-168.
102.   Sergeant Randy McIntyre, Johnson County Sheriff's Department,
        interview with the author, 12 December 2007.
102.   Deputy Alan Harris, Johnson County Sheriff's Department,
        interview with the author, 12 December 2007.